TABLE OF CONTENTS

③

TABLE OF CONTENTS

This book is dedicated to all those who lost their way and
inspired me to help others find theirs. I also wish
to thank those authors whose works are listed in the
Bibliography, without those insights, my own
understanding of the subject would have been
considerably lessened.

Lee Elston

SQUARE PEGS & ROUND HOLES

HOW TO MATCH THE PERSONALITY TO THE JOB

LEE ELSTON

Published by Alexander Associates
4 South Street, Fowey, Cornwall Pl23 IAR. UK.

In the USA, First Step Enterprises
PO Box 87265 San Diego, Cal. 92138-7265 USA.

First Published 1984
Reprinted 1986
Second Edition 1995

ISBN 1 899526 50 1

Occasionally one meets a person whose work is his joy, or as the late Joseph Campbell put it, one who is "following his bliss". But that happens all too seldom in the western world. Here people seem to be more concerned with getting "bigger and better" everything – incomes, houses, cars, fame, even notoriety!

Those persons who are truly successful must be those who are using their primary function in earning their living. One thinks of the school teacher who said his favourite part of each day was when he was in the classroom. He certainly was an extraverted intuitive feeling type. In my counselling experience and in everyday observation of my fellow human beings in their working environments, I see all too many who are striving after the success symbols of our society, whether or not going after them is giving them joy.

One problem that occurs when an individual is trying to earn a living, using his/her inferior function, is the effect on other people. How many of us have been put off our restaurant meal by a cranky waiter or waitress? Thinking function operating in a feeling function job? Some of us may have had a bolt left unfastened when a tire was changed, resulting in almost losing a wheel; an intuitive doing a sensation person's job, perhaps? The list is endless, the examples legion.

It is gratifying to know that I am not alone in recognising the importance of the psyche's primary function, as it operates in the principal occupation of most people's lives that of earning a living. Hopefully, more and more career counsellors, personnel directors and employment advisers will become cognisant of this principle and guide our working population toward a life filled with job satisfaction and joy.

by Robert A. Johnson
Leucadia, California, USA

It has been just over ten years since *Square Pegs & Round Holes* was first published, since when it has been read and used by thousands, in schools and businesses. What has been gratifying to me has been how the PREFERENTIAL QUESTIONNAIRE has been used to discover an individual's psychological type, the knowledge of which has not only helped numerous people in selecting a career, but has also helped resolve differences between individuals in families and organisations. With a knowledge of 'type' differences, husbands and wives have begun to understand each other instead of blame; parents have started to appreciate their children rather than criticise; co-workers have learned to value each others' approach to a problem rather than be antagonistic or combative.'

A few years ago I gave a talk on C. G. Jung's theory of *Psychological Types* to a group of unmarried, middle-aged people. The audience was attentive and I answered many questions at the end of the talk. A week or so later, I met a man who had been in attendance. He told me that on returning home after my talk, he had telephoned his brother to whom he had not spoken for thirty years. As he had listened to me describe the sixteen (psychological types) of personality and how the four functions (thinking, feeling, intuition and sensation) worked; how individuals reacted very differently to the same situation, often resulting in members of the same family, because of their 'type' differences misunderstanding each other; he had suddenly gained an insight into his brother and why they had come to a 'parting of the ways' so long ago. He told me they were planning to meet in a few days time. He now understood, why they had differed so bitterly and he was looking forward to reconciliation. This revelation came about after only a brief introduction to 'type' differences.

Credit must be given to the *Myer-Briggs Type Indicator* which was one of the first instruments used to identify an individual's psychological type. It is used by many organisations, schools and counsellors, especially in the USA.

Unfortunately, it can only be administered by an approved, trained person and is therefore not readily available to the general public. A knowledge of one's psychological type need not be esoteric. It can be known after the *truthful* response to a few situational questions. The result can be reconciling, healing and enlightening.

I am not alone in my conviction about psychological 'types'. "If you had done nothing else but given us your book, *Psychological Types* and made us capable of speaking at last a common psychological language, you would have done enough."* That is what Laurens van der Post said to Dr Carl Gustav Jung. I certainly agree with him.

I look forward to this second edition of *Square Pegs & Round Holes* being used by people of all ages and all walks of life; not only to assist them in discovering the kind of work or profession in which they may find satisfaction and fulfilment but also to gain self-knowledge, and an understanding and tolerance of others.

With this edition *Square Pegs & Round Holes* is being published for the first time in Great Britain with 'British' spelling. As there is an occasional difference in job titles the American version has been put in brackets.

Lee Elston
Cornwall, UK, 1995.

* Van der post, Laurens, *Jung & the Story of Our Time* Penguin Books, 1978, pg. 192.

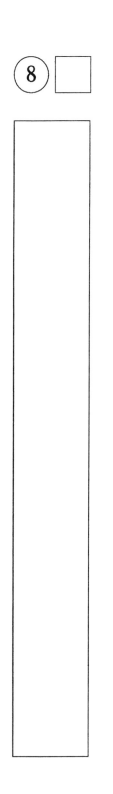

8

Several years ago, I taught a class to adults entitled 'Vocational Orientation'. Its purpose was to teach the techniques necessary to apply for and get a job.

The class was structured in such a way that each student had the opportunity to view him/herself in an interview situation on a closed circuit TV, first at the beginning of the course and then again after thirty hours of instruction. After the first and last videoed 'interview', we looked at each presentation and analysed the behaviour, responses and appearance of the interviewees.

After instruction, there was a remarkable difference in the way the interview situation was handled. In almost every case there was an obvious improvement in the level of self-esteem and ability to make a positive impression on an interviewer.

The one observable quality that makes the greatest difference between the employable and the unemployable person in an interview situation can be summed up in the word 'enthusiasm'. When the class considered what an employer looks for in a potential employee, in addition to the necessary skills and perhaps, experience, it was agreed that loyalty, an ability to get along with others, maturity, reliability and a willingness to work for something more than a pay cheque were desirable qualities. All of these qualities could be summed up in the word, 'enthusiasm'. The question then arose, how is it possible to find and get the kind of job where one will want to be loyal, co-operative, reliable and full of enthusiasm? How can one be sure what kind of job that is? It appears that it is only a matter of luck.

I have observed however, that most people who are what is called a 'success' in their field, are also people who are happy in their work. Somehow they have stumbled into the right profession, one apparently made for them. But is this correct? Is it only a matter of luck or could there be some reason for it? It is my firm belief that although it seems that it is just 'luck', in reality it is because the job or profession and the individual's psychological 'type' fit.

A knowledge of one's psychological type can be of assistance when making a career choice and/or commencing on an educational training programme. Included as a part of the curriculum in the Vocational Orientation class was my PREFERENTIAL QUESTIONNAIRE, a series of questions/ situations structured, as to identify the psychological type. It showed which of the four functions of the psyche, thinking, feeling, sensation or intuition, a person used easily and whether the person was introverted or extraverted. Those terms were first used by the Swiss psychiatrist, Dr C. G. Jung.

Dr Jung came to his theory of psychological types in an attempt to understand his differences with his friend and mentor, Dr Sigmund Freud. Dr. Jung observed, while listening to his patients, how similar life situations would be viewed and acted upon in totally different ways by different people. He puzzled as to why. His conclusions are written in *Psychological Types*, published in 1923.

He observed how some of his patients seemed to relate to the world of people, events and objects occurring outside themselves. They responded with action. These persons seemed to get energy through their contact with other people and the outer world. This attitude Jung called 'Extraversion' **(E)**. Other of his patients, he noted, seemed to relate more to what could be termed their 'inner world'. They were more interested in the world of ideas. They spent more time reflecting on what was happening, or had happened.

They seemed to receive energy when they shut the door on the outside world and withdrew into themselves. This attitude he termed 'Introversion' **(I)**.

Some gathered information about the world through the use of their five senses. This function he called 'Sensation' **(S)**. Others seem to just "know". This unseen, unprovable faculty, this 'knowing' he labelled 'Intuition' **(N)**. These two functions of the psyche he called the 'Perceptive' **(P)** functions.

Some people placed a value on what they experienced in terms of whether it was rational, logical and true. Those people viewed their world, the people and events in it analytically, critically and objectively. They used what Jung called their 'Thinking' **(T)** function. Others put emphasis on the human element, viewing people and events sympathetically, considering kindness and co-operation of primary value. They viewed their world, the people and events in it, subjectively. This function of the psyche he called 'Feeling' **(F)**. These two valuing functions, Thinking and Feeling, he labelled 'Judging' **(J)** functions. The average individual will have developed strongly only *one* perceiving function and *one* judging function. Either thinking *or* feeling, the judging functions; sensation *or* intuition, the perceiving functions will be primary, but will be assisted by one function in the other category.

All the functions – sensation, intuition, thinking and feeling, exist in everyone; but the degree that each function is used determines the temperament, the 'personality' of an individual.

A good analogy is right or left-handedness; most of us have two hands. We use one effortlessly, the other with great difficulty. The same is true with the functions of the psyche; one function – the primary one – is used effortlessly, it is like breathing, the secondary – auxiliary – one helps. But for an individual to try and earn a living using his/her inferior function – the least developed function – is like right-handed persons trying to write, draw or eat with their left hand. American author and psychologist, Robert A. Johnson wrote, "One should never try to earn one's living with the inferior function" *. When a person knows which function is used naturally and effortlessly, it is much easier to find the kind of work in which he or she may find job satisfaction and achieve happiness.

I remember one of my students, a thirty-five year old man, who had always worked as a typist. In the first practice interview, he was 'applying' for a job as a typist. As he talked about "why he wanted the job", his voice lacked animation, there was no vitality in his posture or sparkle in his eye. In other words, he lacked "enthusiasm". After he took the PREFERENTIAL QUESTIONNAIRE he discovered he was an **ISFJ** (Introvert, Sensation, Feeling, Judging). When I spoke with him about the results, he acknowledged he never liked being a typist. He said he would prefer working directly with people where he could see that what he did really mattered; that some way his work could improve the quality of someone's life. He realised that he needed to move into a profession that was focused on helping people, where he wouldn't have to be dealing with mechanical equipment and where there weren't too many distractions.

A few weeks after the close of the class, I received a letter from him, telling me he had started training to be a physiotherapist, a field where he would be working directly with people in a nurturing way. He wrote, "Thank you for changing my life." Of course, I didn't change his life. He did. But a knowledge of his type helped to give him the impetus and the courage to do something about changing direction.

Another example is of a young man whose principle job involved sitting in an office answering the telephone. He told me that whenever there was an errand to be run, he was always the first to volunteer. He needed to get away from the desk where he felt stifled. After completing the PREFERENTIAL QUESTIONNAIRE he discovered he was an **ENFP** – (Extravert, Intuitive, Feeling, Perceptive). Then h knew why he liked to be the one to run the errands and why he wasn't happy in an office situation. He decided that what he really wanted to do was to be a travelling salesman. He commented, "Answering these questions and seeing the results, gives me permission to be who I am!"

I think most employers would agree that they would choose happy, enthusiastic employees, in preference to those with a 'Thank God it's Friday' attitude about their work. But how to achieve it? One way, is to be sure to hire people who know who they are and what they like to do; what they do without stress. Try to suit the personality of the individual to the job and the job to the personality of the applicant.

Students looking forward to future careers; women returning to work after several years absence or perhaps going to work for the first time; men, having to change careers after redundancy; all are searching for their ideal place in the world of work. If wise, they will seek work that not only will give them a pay cheque, but also an occupation that will fulfil them personally, making them enthusiastic, happy employees. Perhaps they will choose to be self-employed. A knowledge of their psychological/ personality type can start them off on the right track, thus saving time, money and possible heartache.

In order to facilitate this, use the PREFERENTIAL QUESTIONNAIRE, a series of seventy-four questions and/or situations to which **there is no right, wrong, good or bad answer**. How the questions are answered will, however, give a good indication as to which of the four functions are used effortlessly and whether the energy impetus is toward extraversion or introversion.

A potential employer will naturally require skill and/or aptitude tests and an interview before commitment and decision, but as an indicator of the type of position in a firm where an individual will be most productive, the use of the PREFERENTIAL QUESTIONNAIRE can prove helpful.

Students, after discovering their type, can be guided into those subjects that will be most useful in preparing them for future work; anyone seeking work can use it to assist them in finding a career or a job where they can be relatively stress-free. The PREFERENTIAL QUESTIONNAIRE has been informally measured by the author against the Myer-Briggs Type Indicator *(2) with her own counsellees, students and seminar participants and similar results have been reached in the majority of cases. It should be used, however, as a guide, to help in making individual, critical decisions. This book has been written to be helpful, not definitive.

When the day comes and we are all 'whole' with the conscious use of all four of our functions and are equally well balanced in introverted and extraverted attitudes, the need for help will no longer be necessary. But until that day arrives, any help to assist in discovering who we are and what we want to do can not help but be useful.

To that end, this book is written.

*(1) Robert Johnson, *Ecstasy*, Harper & Row, SanFrancisco, 1987 Pg. 56.

*(2) Katherine C. Briggs & Isabel Briggs Myers, *MyerBriggs Type Indicator*, Consulting Psychologists Press, 7 College Ave. Palo Alto, 1978.

Note. Throughout this book I have used the spelling 'extraversion' deliberately, as that is how the word was originally used by Dr Jung. You will find the *primary* function for each personality type has been **in bold print** in the headings.

Throughout the text the following letters are often used instead of the entire word Extraversion (**E**); Introversion (**I**); Thinking (**T**); Feeling (**F**); Sensation (**S**); Intuition (**N**); Judgement (**J**); Perceptive (**P**)

☐ ⑮

PREFERENTIAL QUESTIONNAIRE

Remove answer sheet from the back of the book
Read the following situations/questions and tick the 'A' or 'B'
column that is your **FIRST** reaction. If you have difficulty in
deciding, *do not answer. Remember there is NO CORRECT OR
INCORRECT, GOOD OR BAD* answer.
Answer what is TRUE for you!

1. You are to attend a party where you will know no one.
You
a. *look forward to the opportunity to meet lots of new people.*
b. *wonder how long you will have to stay before you can leave.*

2. It's a rainy day. You have some free time to watch TV.
You would prefer to watch
a. *a sporting event or soap.*
b. *a interview/political analysis/or art discussion.*

3. You
a. *usually remember where you put things.*
b. *often forget where you put things.*

4. You want to buy a new car. It is more important to
a. *analyse the facts and figures.*
b. *fall in love with it.*

5. It is a greater fault to be
a. *too sympathetic.*
b. *too critical.*

6. When you shop for clothes, you are more apt to
a. *be very careful, going to many stores comparing prices
and value.*
b. *be rather impulsive, buying at the first store you enter.*

(16)

7. You have said you would do something or go somewhere at a certain time. You are
a. *comfortable with your decision.*
b. *uncomfortable and wish you could change your mind.*

8. In a crowd of people, you are more likely
a. *to be unaware of people looking at you.*
b. *to be aware of people looking at you.*

9. You would be willing to work especially hard in order to
a. *have more luxuries and a "better life."*
b. *have the chance to become famous for your work.*

10. Which group of words do you find more appealing?
a. *matter-of-fact, decisive, realistic.*
b. *imaginative, impulsive, idealistic.*

11. In describing yourself, you would be more apt to say
a. *"My head rules my heart."*
b. *"My heart rules my head."*

12. Which school subject did/do you find more interesting?
a. *mathematics.*
b. *history.*

13. If you have a choice, you prefer your activities to be
a. *planned.*
b. *on the spur of the moment.*

14. You are in the middle of moving when you decide that a plant would look just perfect in a certain spot. You would
a. *finish what you started and then get the plant.*
b. *stop what you are doing and get the plant immediately.*

15. You feel that most people find you
a. *easy to know.*
b. *hard to know.*

16. You are more apt to be called a
a. *"stick in the mud."*
b. *"a rolling stone that gathers no moss."*

17. You have won a prize book. You would prefer a book on
a. *cooking or carpentry.*
b. *astrology or psychology.*

18. If you were a judge sentencing in a court of law, you would be more likely to take into consideration
a. *the law.*
b. *the circumstances.*

19. In dealing with people, you feel it is more important to be
a. *always truthful.*
b. *always kind.*

20. You're leaving on holiday by car in the morning. You are awake at 3:00 a.m. You would
a. *wait until morning to leave.*
b. *get up, get dressed and get going.*

21. You almost always
a. *finish what you have to do on schedule or even a bit ahead of time.*
b. *finish just "under the wire," a bit late, or perhaps not at all.*

22. You express your feelings more comfortably
a. *outloud.*
b. *in writing.*

23. If you were being cast in a play, which role would be better "type-casting"?
a. *organised business leader.*
b. *absent-minded professor.*

24. Regarding your body, you are more apt to
a. *take good care of it.*
b. *tend to ignore it, figuring it will take care of itself.*

25. You have some free time to attend a lecture.
You would be more apt to attend a
a. *lecture on scientific issues of the day.*
b. *lecture on "How to Win Friends & Influence People".*

26. You have a business of your own. There is an employee
who is always late to work because of family matters.
You would be more apt to
a. *fire the person and hire someone who will put in a full
day's work.*
b. *be understanding and try to work something out.*

27. As an employee you prefer to work according to
a. *the rules of the organisation.*
b. *your own rules.*

28. You would prefer as a friend one whose attitude about
money is
a. *"a penny saved is a penny earned."*
b. *"easy come, easy go."*

29. When the phone rings at your home and there are other
members of the family present, you
a. *hope to be the first to answer it.*
b. *hope someone else will get to it first.*

30. You are planning a trip to a place you have never been.
You prefer
a. *going with a tour group.*
b. *going with only a guide book.*

31. A new business is opening in your neighbourhood. You need a job. They are hiring in all departments. You would be more interested in a position in
a. *production and sales.*
b. *research and design.*

32. Among all the people you know, would you say there are more
a. *you don't like?*
b. *you do like?*

33. You are a teacher. A student asks you to let him take a test before scheduled so he can leave early to go on holiday with a friend. It is against the school policy, but you have the authority to make an exception. It is better to
a. *abide by school policy.*
b. *be kind to the student.*

34. You
a. *always write your social engagements on a calendar or in a diary to which you refer daily.*
b. *find keeping a social calendar/diary uncomfortable and stifling, but if you do keep one you often fail to look at it.*

35. You prefer to work
a. *to deadlines.*
b. *when you feel like it.*

36. You have a day off. You are more apt to
a. *call a friend and go somewhere.*
b. *stay home alone.*

37. You prefer as friends those who have
a. *common sense.*
b. *imagination.*

20

38. You are more apt to trust your
a. *experience.*
b. *hunch.*

39. You prefer to associate with people who are
a. *logical and realistic.*
b. *sympathetic and kind.*

40. You
a. *seldom get your feelings hurt.*
b. *often get your feelings hurt.*

41. You prefer to associate with people who
a. *prefer to make their plans ahead of time.*
b. *will drop everything and be ready to go at a moment's notice.*

42. If entertaining, you prefer people
a. *not to come unless they have been invited.*
b. *to just drop in and take whatever is going.*

43. On a job, you prefer to work
a. *with lots of people around.*
b. *by yourself with few distractions.*

44. You would be more likely to enroll in a class on
a. *upholstering, dressmaking, household or automotive repairs.*
b. *psychology, comparative religions, creative writing or astrology.*

45. On your day off from work/school you have two invitations. One is to go to attend a sporting event; the other is to a new show at an art gallery. Which would you accept?
a. *The sporting event.*
b. *The art show.*

46. There has been an accident on the job. Your first impulse is to
a. *figure out what went wrong, then try and correct it.*
b. *see if anyone was hurt.*

47. You would rather be thought of as
a. *always fair.*
b. *always kind.*

48. Which group of words do you find more appealing?
a. *orderly, punctual, permanent.*
b. *easy-going, leisurely, changeable.*

49. You find that you make decisions
a. *quickly and easily.*
b. *slowly and with some difficulty.*

50. You are offered temporary employment in a department store. You may choose between two available jobs. You would prefer
a. *to serve food to the public.*
b. *to wrap packages by yourself.*

51. You travel a certain distance by car each day. You generally
a. *always go the same way.*
b. *try to find as many different ways to go as possible.*

52. You enjoy being with
a. *realistic people.*
b. *imaginative people.*

53. Which groups of words do you find more appealing?
a. *firm, analytical, convincing.*
b. *gentle, sympathetic, touching.*

54. On a job, in which department would you prefer to work?
a. *equipment repairs.*
b. *customer complaints.*

(22)

55. When you get up in the morning on a day when you are not committed to work or school, you

a. *know exactly what you're going to do all day.*

b. *let the day "just happen".*

56. How would most people describe you?

a. *serious and reliable.*

b. *light hearted and easy-going.*

57. You find it necessary to write an important personal letter. You

a. *just sit down and "do it".*

b. *take time to really think through what it is you're going to say.*

58. You have inherited some money. You would be more inclined to

a. *buy something that will increase in value.*

b. *take a trip.*

59. If you are visiting a new city you would be more likely to enjoy

a. *going shopping.*

b. *visiting a local museum.*

60. You are more influenced by a news story that

a. *is factual and realistic.*

b. *touches your heart.*

61. If you were or are a teacher, you feel that

a. *the subject matter is more important than the student.*

b. *the student is more important than the subject matter.*

62. You are most comfortable when you have

a. *your time arranged and accounted for.*

b. *lots of free time to do as you like.*

63. If you have a number of things that need to be done. You will most likely
a. make a list.
b. trust to luck.

64. Someone is planning a party in your honour. You would rather it be a
a. "big bash" with almost everyone you know.
b. quiet party with just a few very special friends.

65. You have received a substantial amount of money. You would be most apt to
a. invest it.
b. buy something beautiful or take a holiday.

66. You think of shopping as
a. entertaining.
b. necessary.

67. You've a drawer that won't open. Something is apparently stuck. Your immediate response is
a. to think, "What went in must come out" and figure out what to do.
b. tug, pull, and get frustrated.

68. It is wiser to
a. tell the unkind truth.
b. tell the kind lie.

69. On personal projects you
a. almost always complete what you start.
b. frequently do not complete what you start.

70. Which saying is more appealing to you?
a. "A job worth doing is worth doing well."
b. "A man on his galloping horse will never know the difference."

(24)

71. During a conversation, if someone interrupts you
a. *hardly notice it.*
b. *get quite annoyed.*

72. If attending a party where games are being played, you would be more apt to join in with those playing
a. *bridge.*
b. *charades.*

73. You have an idea for a new business. You discover someone has a similar plan. Your first inclination would be to
a. *see the other person as a competitor.*
b. *see how you and the other person could work together.*

74. A planned routine
a. *appeals to you.*
b. *frustrates you.*

Directions for Scoring

Count up the number of ticks in each column. Add the ticks in column 1 and in column 2. Total the ticks in columns 3 & 5; 4 & 6; 7 & 9; 8 & 10; 11 & 13; 12 & 14.

If there are:
More ticks in column "1" ....= **E**
More ticks in column "2" ....= **I**
More ticks in column "3 & 5" ....= **S**
More ticks in column "4 & 6" ....= **N**
More ticks in column "7 & 9" ....= **T**
More ticks in column "8 & 10" ....= **F**
More ticks in column "11 & 13" ....= **J**
More ticks in column "12 & 14" ....= **P**

After finding which 'type' you are, locate the description of your psychological type and 'suggested' career choices on the following pages.

Note: Your *primary function* will be in **BOLD PRINT**.

(26)

I would like to emphasise that the following lists of potential jobs/careers are only 'suggested'. The 1991 edition of the US *Dictionary of Occupational Titles* was in 4 volumes averaging over 1000 pages in each one. Obviously, it was Impossible to analyse all of them. Every year there are new occupations and many jobs are eliminated as automation takes the place of man-power in many industries. It is important, that you consider the basic description of your type, know your strengths and weaknesses and how they apply to the world of work. Please do not consider my 'suggested careers' as limiting.

TOP DOG

You are a natural leader and administrator. If you are not in charge you will be constantly frustrated because you always see a better, more efficient way of doing just about anything.

Therefore, it is absolutely necessary that you be in a position where you can put your ideas into effect and give the orders. Otherwise, you may make yourself and others very unhappy as you go around telling them how they 'ought' to do something. You are probably right, but it works best if you're in a situation where you are listened to!

You are a very disciplined, conscientious, reliable, work-oriented individual. There's probably not a better administrator anywhere around, especially in the fields of business, education or government. But you need to learn to relax and play.

Your greatest danger is that you may unintentionally hurt someone's feelings, because the fact that people have feelings is something you may overlook. When you learn to take life a bit less seriously, to 'live and let live,' you have the potential to become an unforgettable leader. A former lady British Prime Minister is undoubtedly of this type.

Please avoid any kind of menial, monotonous tasks or any occupation where it is important that you please people, i.e. sales!

DESCRIPTIVE WORDS: Executive, commanding, objective, efficient, logical, rational, structured, orderly, dutiful, goal-oriented, punctual, disciplined, empirical, analytical, work-oriented, serious.

Suggested Careers for **ENTJ'S**

Academic Dean
Advertising Account Executive
Agricultural Economist
Architect
Archeologist
Athletic Director
Banking/ all kinds- any level
Barrister (Attorney)
Business Consultant
Business Manager
Cardiologist
Chartered Surveyor
    (Real Estate Appraiser)
Chemist
City Editor
City/County Councillor
    (Manager)
College/University Dean
Computer Programmer
Consumer Affairs Director
Contract Specialist
Corporate Benefits Manager
Credit Union Manager
Data-Processing Manager
Design Engineer
Economist
Economic Geographer
Economic Development Field
Economic Analyst
Employment Supervisor
Emergency Specialist
Engineer
Explorer
Financial Adviser
Film Producer

Film Director
Fire Chief
Finance Company Manager
Geologist
Health Services
Administrator
Headmaster (School
Principal)
Head Public Librarian
Hospital Administrator
Hospital Purchasing Director
Hotel Manager
Industrial Editor
Information Manager
Information Marketing
Manager
Information Processor
Insurance Sales Underwriter
Internist
Judge
Labour Relations Consultant
Law Enforcement Director
Management Analyst
Manufacturing Engineer
Market Analyst
Mathematician
Medical Technologist
Metallographer
Metallurgical Engineer
Meteorologist
Microbiologist
Military Services–Officer
Mineralogist
Mining Engineer
Mycologist

Naval Architect
Nematologist
Neurologist
Neuropharmacologist
News Analyst
News Assistant
Newspaper Editor
Newspaper Editorial Writer
News Reporter
Nuclear Engineer
Oceanographer
Parasitologist
Political Scientist
Politician
Prime Minister (President)
Patent Attorney
Pathologist
Petroleum Engineer
Pharmacologist
Physical Anthropologist
Physicist
Physiologist
Plastics Engineer
Pollution Control Engineer
Production Engineer
Production Planning
Supervisor
Project Engineer

Psychiatrist
Psychologist
Public Finance Specialist
Purchasing Analyst
Purchasing Manager
Quality Control Engineer
Rate & Cost Analyst
Rate Supervisor
Records Analyst Manager
Research Mathematician
Safety Engineer
Schedule Planning Manager
School Financial-Aid Officer
Seismologist
Systems Analyst
Sociologist
Soil Scientist
Solicitor (Attorney)
Space Physicist
Statistician
TV Programme Manager
TV News Broadcaster/Analyst
TV. Interviewer
Theatre Administrator
Theatre Director
University President
Urban Sociologist
Wage & Salary Administrator

PEOPLE PLEASER

If all the teachers of the world were like you, there would be a lot of happy students. Your enthusiasm, care and insight inspire others, and inspiring others is what makes you happiest. You have an easy facility with language, and may prefer speaking to writing.

You are attracted to new ideas and theories and your natural enthusiasm makes you a very good salesperson. You also have a flair for making others feel comfortable and at home, and can do well in an occupation where this quality is important.

Your greatest weakness is your tendency to get bored with a project or job after the problems are solved. In other words, you are more a pioneer than a settler! You need challenge and variety in your work. Because you are often unaware of your body's needs, you may find that it breaks down when you get over tired.

You could be considered a dilettante, because of what may be your superficial knowledge about a lot of things, but your charm and warm-hearted attitude will win friends anyway. You are at your best working in a situation where there is very little direct supervision. An **ENFJ** must lead or at least not be bossed!

You need to feel free to 'do your own thing'. Be careful not to jump to conclusions without checking all the facts, and try to be around compatible people.

You must avoid any routine, clerical or mechanical work. You like a challenge and a lot of variety.

DESCRIPTIVE TERMS: Leader, enthusiastic, optimistic, co-operative, caring, trustworthy, even-tempered, hospitable, verbal, catalytic, friendly.

Suggested Careers for ENFJ'S

Actor
Advertising Sales Representative
Advertising Manager
Airline Lounge Receptionist
Airline Hostess
Art Director
Artist's Agent
Broadcasting Director
Broadcast-Secretary
Business Agent
Career Counsellor
Casework Supervisor
Charity Administrator
Child Psychologist
Clergy Member
Consumer Services Consultant
Dance Therapist
Day Care Centre/Worker
Dean of Students
Dietetics Instructor
Dietician Administrator
Educational Audio-Visual Field
Educational Consultant Specialist
Educational Psychologist
Educational Course Representative
Educational Therapist
Educational Supervisor
Educator, any level, any subject
Employment Counsellor
Employment Agency Manager
Employment Supervisor
Employment Interviewer
Fashion Co-ordinator
Financial Services Sales Agent
Film Producer/Director

Foreign Student Adviser
Group Insurance Sales Agent
Group Leader (Social Services)
Guidance Counsellor
Geriatric Social Worker
Headmaster/mistress
Health Services Administrator
Industrial Sociologist
Homeopathic Physician
Hotel Manager
House Master
Insurance Agent
Internist
Insurance Sales
Instructor/any level, any subject
Representative
Labour Union Business Agent
Labour Relations Consultant
Literary Agent
Life Insurance Sales Agent
Solicitor (Attorney)
Lobbyist
Museum Exhibit Designer
Modelling Instructor
Music Therapist
News Reporter
Newspaper Editor
Marketing Director
Nursing Home Social Worker
Nursing Home Supervisor
Orientation & Mobility
Therapist
Occupational Therapist
Passenger Service Representative
Pediatrician

Personal Manager
Personnel Administrator
Psychologist
Political Science Professor
Political Scientist
Politician
Probation Officer
Psychiatrist
Psychiatric Social Worker
Public Health Educator
Public Relations
Representative
Estate Agent (Real Estate Agent)
Recreation Leader
Recreational Therapist.
Religious Activities Director
School Medical Specialist
Sales Director
Sales Manager

Sales Representative
Social Worker
Social Director
Social Psychologist
Social Group Worker
Sociologist
Social Service Director
Stage Manager
Special Education Director
Teacher's Aide
Summer Camp Director
Television/Theatre
Director/Producer
Theatre Arts Teacher
Urban Sociologist
Travel Agent
Welfare Director
Wedding Consultant

EXECUTIVE

You're just what the doctor ordered. You can captain the ship, put people, things, and activities in order and tune them with an efficiency that is what every organisation of any size needs, and needs very much. You not only can organise and run an enterprise with precision, you are also able to eliminate from the picture anyone who is not doing their job or pulling their weight. You can discipline or fire a person if necessary. You strongly dislike slip-shod, inefficient ways or people. Since you are very realistic and practical, you cannot be convinced by anything that is not logical, well thought out and reasonable. You set your goal, then organise people, things, and events to accomplish it, and on schedule. Your biggest problem is that you may fail to take other people's feelings into account. Others may not see things the same way you do and you may appear to them to be cold-blooded and heartless. Remember that 'feelings are facts'. Learn to give appreciation to others, and you will find you can have the most efficient, smoothly running, office, department, ship, regiment or business anywhere about. Because you believe in living according to the rules, in fact, prefer that the rules be set down and abided by, you can work very well in an 'establishment' kind of job, e.g. the military, law enforcement, government, or in a large office, corporation or factory. You can also be happy working with any kind of machine or with numbers! Please avoid any occupation where it is important that you please people or have to make them happy – sales for example. Leave that to others!

DESCRIPTIVE WORDS: Responsible, punctual, community-minded, traditional, dutiful, realistic, matter-of-fact, organised, orderly, obedient, loyal, conservative, neat, dependable, consistent.

Suggested Careers for ESTJ's

Accountant
Aircraft Electronic Instruments
  Inspector
Airline Schedule Analyst
Airport Security
Airline Pilot
Ammunitions Safety Inspector
Airline Dispatcher
Airline Ramp Agent
Airport Manager
Apartment Building
Superintendent
Appraiser
Auditor
Automobile, Service Manager
Banking, any department,
  any position.
Bookkeeper
Brokerage Manager
Brokerage Clerk
Bursar
Cabinet Maker
Carpenter
Coding Clerk Supervisor
Construction Industry, any
  position, any job
Corrections officer
Credit Analyst
Computer Operator
Computer Programmer
Court Clerk
Credit Collection Supervisor
Customs-Import Specialist
Customs Inspector
Data Base Manager

Data Control Supervisor
Data Typist
Dental Laboratory Manager
Department Store Manager
Document Examiner
Department Store Manager
Electrician
Electronic communications
  personnel
Estate Agent (Real Estate Agent)
Fireman
Geo-thermal Power Plant
Supervisor
Grocery Store Manager
Harbour Master
Health Officer
Health Care Facility Inspector
Highway Contractor
Highway Inspector
Hospital Administrator
Hotel Manager
Import/Export Agent
Internal Revenue Agent
Law Enforcement Officer
Legal Assistant
Legal Secretary
Legislative Reporter
Logistics Engineer
Machine Operator
Market Analyst
Mechanical Inspector
Medical Administrator
Medical Records Clerk
Medical Secretary
Military Services (any role)

Mine Superintendent
Micrographics Service Supervisor
Natural Gas Utilisation Manager
Oceanographer
Office Manager
Occupational Safety and Health Inspector
Oil-well Services Supervisor
Optician
Patent Attorney
Pawn Broker
Personal Manager
Pollster
Probate Solicitor
Production Control Supervisor
Production Engineer
Project Engineer
Public Finance Expert

Pharmacist
Proof Reader
Purchasing Agent
Quality Control Coordinator
Rate & Cost Analyst
Railway Worker
Shipping & Receiving Clerk
Solicitor (Attorney)
Statistical Clerk
Stockroom Supervisor
Surveyor (Real Estate Appraiser)
Tax Accountant
Television, Film, Radio, Theatre Producer
Trust Evaluation Clerk
Wage & Salary Administrator
Water-Treatment Plan Manager
Warehouse Manager
Wholesaler

ESFJ – EXTRAVERT, SENSATION, FEELING, JUDGEMENT

SUPER SALESPERSON

You are the natural nurturer, radiating harmony, good will, friendliness, sympathy and caring. When there are good 'vibes' in your environment, you work well with loyalty and perseverance. But if the 'vibes' are bad, your work can be affected even to the point where you will quit. As an executive, you are very good, with others liking to work for and with you. It is very important that you feel appreciated, for if you feel criticised, you tend to draw back within yourself and your work suffers.

Because of your natural good will towards others, you do best when working in any person-to-person job, e.g., selling, teaching, supervising, or nursing. You enjoy talking with people, even over the telephone.

Because you like and adapt easily to a routine, either to one you have made up for yourself or one you have been given, you may suffer if your routine is interrupted. Your work is orderly and neat. A place for everything and every-thing in its place may well be a description of your philosophy.

You may get in trouble because you do something the way you feel it should be done without checking first. You may also have a tendency to let your sociability slow you down on a job. Remember to be brief and business like when that is what is called for and leave the socialising for after work hours. Unless, of course, your work calls for being friendly and outgoing - selling for example.

You are the most practical and materialistic of all the types and are able to adjust yourself to outer realities. You can discipline yourself physically and you enjoy physical activity for its own sake.

Please avoid any occupation where your friendly, happy, outgoing nature will not be appreciated.

DESCRIPTIVE WORDS: Friendly, caring, conscientious, responsible, nurturing, orderly, sociable, outgoing, loyal, sympathetic, emotional, responsive, obedient, stable, traditional, sentimental, soft-hearted, materialistic.

Suggested Careers for ESFJ'S

Accountant	Dietician
Agricultural-Business Agent	Directory Assistance Operator
Airline Pilot	Disc Jockey
Airline Lounge Receptionist	Druggist
Airline Flight Attendant	Educational Attendance Clerk
Anaesthesiologist	Educational Audio-Visual Advisor
Art Director	Endodontist
Art Teacher	Elementary School Teacher
Automobile Dealer	Executive Secretary
Automobile Driving Instructor	Farm Equipment Dealer
Bank Teller	Exercise Physiologist
Barber/Hair Stylist	Estate Agent (Real Estate Agent)
Biologist	Farm Management Advisor
Blood Bank Technician	Fashion Design Teacher
Bookkeeper	Fashion Photographer
Brokerage Manager	Fire Protection Engineer
Bus Station Manager	Food & Beverage Manager
Creche Attendant	Foreign Exchange Clerk
Child Psychologist	Food Broker
Chiropractor	Foreign Student Advisor
Circulation Manager	Foreign Exchange Teller
Club Manager	Funeral Director
Classified Ad Clerk	Front Office Hotel Manager
Conference Typist	Garden Centre Manager
Consumer Financial Advisor	Fund Raising Director
Corrective Physical Therapist	Geriatric Psychologist
Cosmetologist	Geriatric Nurse
Credit Collections Secretary	Geriatric Social Worker
Credit Counsellor	Golf Club Manager
Customer Service Representative	Grain Broker
Dental Assistant	Hair Stylist, Hairdresser
Dental Hygienist	Health Club Attendant
Dentist	Hobby Shop Manager
Dermatologist	Health Club Manager
Dialysis Technician	Health Service Worker

Health Record Administrator
Home Economist
Hospital Central Supply Clerk
Hospital Admitting Clerk
Hospital Food Service Admin.
Immigration Lawyer
Industrial Arts Teacher
Industrial Cafeteria Manager
Information Clerk
Inhalation Therapist
Interior Designer
Labour Union Business Agent
Librarian
Legal Secretary
Loan Interviewer
Lobbyist
Make-up Artist
Manual Arts Therapist
Masseur/Masseuse
Mathematics Teacher
Media Clerk
Medical Assistant
Medical Secretary
Medical Records Clerk
Medical Office Receptionist
Medical Records Administrator
Medical Technologist
Mental Health Technician
Midwife
Mobile Canteen Operator
Modelling Instructor
Music Therapist
Parole Officer
Naturopathic Physician
Nurse
Nursing Assistant (Aide)
Nursing Home Recreational

Director
Nutritionist
Occupational Therapist
Office Clerk
Office Manager
Office Nurse
Ophthalmologist
Optician
Optometrist
Oral Pathologist
Oral Surgeon
Order Clerk
Order Dept. Supervisor
Orthodontist
Passenger Service Representative
Personal Assistant
Private Secretary
Pediatrician
Physical Education Teacher
Physiotherapist
Playroom Attendant
Primary School Teacher
Psychiatric Social Worker
Psychiatrist
Psychologist
Publican
Public Health Worker
Public Health Educator
Public Relations
Representative
Radiologist
Radiation Therapist
Receptionist
Reflexologist
Residence Counsellor
Recreational Leader/Therapist
Religious Activities Director

Reservation Clerk
Respiratory Therapist
Sales Representative
Salesperson
School Media Specialist
School Secretary
School Social Worker
School Superintendent
Social Worker
Social Director
Survey Worker
Social Psychologist
Social Services Director
Special Education Teacher
Speech Pathologist
Sports Marketer
Stockbroker

Summer Camp Director
Television Producer
Tax Payer Service Representative
Teacher's Assistant (Aide)
Ticket Agent
Welfare Director
Tourist Information Assistant
Travel Agent
Travel Information Centre
Clerk
Veterinarian Surgeon (Vet)
Wedding Consultant
Waiter/Waitress
Wardrobe Supervisor
Warehousemen/Supervisor
X-Ray Technician

ENTP – EXTRAVERT, INTUITIVE, THINKING, PERCEPTIVE

INVENTOR

If that 'better mousetrap' is ever built, it will be one of you who will have thought up how to do it. If there is a better, more efficient, more practical, or just more ingenious way of doing anything, you will be the one to think of it. Efficiency expert, par excellence! However, you may discover that the people you are trying to convince your way is better may not appreciate your help or ideas. Therefore, make sure you are in a position where your word is law!

You intensely dislike living by anyone's rules but your own, and have been known even to break your own rules if you find a better way or if the old rules have become boring. A challenge is what you like best. You enjoy solving problems, but once the problem is solved, you want to move on. You make good inventors, scientists, teachers, engineers, trouble shooters, mathematicians. Some of the people who were responsible in getting man on the moon were undoubtedly people like you!

If your self-discipline is not developed, you may find that you start a lot of projects, have lots of wonderful ideas, but somehow something always happens so that the idea never takes form. You start out with a lot of enthusiasm, but bog down and give up when the going gets rough.

Let your thinking help you be objective and self-critical, and your objectivity may help you sell your ideas to others.

Please avoid any occupation where living by the rules is necessary, for example – the military. We don't want to see you court-martialled!

DESCRIPTIVE WORDS: Ingenious, challenged, enthusiastic, competent, adaptable, innovative, logical, analytical, easy-going, non-conformist, energetic, charismatic.

Suggested Careers for ENTP's

Adventurer
Anthropologist
Archeologist
Astronomer
Astrologist
Astronaut
Architect
Advertising Account Executive
Barrister (Attorney)
Buyer
Computer Industry –
    Programmer etc
Criminologist
Cryptanalyst
Cyberneticist
Cytologist
Demographer
Dietetic Researcher
Diver
Design Engineer
Detective
Drama Coach
Drilling Engineer
Earth Scientist
Ecologist
Engineer, design, electrical,
    chemical, mechanical etc.
Entomologist
Environmental Engineer
Environmental Scientist
Estate Agent (Real Estate Agent)
Explorer
Geophysicist
Film, TV, Radio Producer/Director
Foreign Correspondent

Geneticist
Geographer
Geologist
Industrial Designer
Industrial Editor
Industrial Engineer
Industrial Health Physicist
Industrial Hygienist
Industrial Microbiologist
Industrial Occupational Analyst
Industrial Pharmacologist
Information Scientist
Information System Programmer
Internist
Intelligence Research
International Lawyer
Investigative Reporter
Journalist
Judge
Labour Relations Consultant
Literary Agent
Lobbyist
Management Analyst
Manufacturing Engineer
Marine Biologist
Marine Ecologist
Marine Meterologist
Marine Geologist
Materials Engineer
Market Research Analyst
Metallurgical Engineer
Microbiologist
Morphologist
Meterologist
Mineralogist

Microwave Engineer
Mining Engineer
Mineral Processing Engineer
Naturopathic Physician
Mycologist
Nematologist
Naval Architect
Neuropharmacologist
Neurologist
Newspaper Columnist
Newspaper Editor
News Analyst
Nuclear Engineer
Nuclear Physicist
Newspaper Editorial Writer
Oceanographer
Ornithologist
Paleontologist
Pathologist
Petroleum Engineer
Physicist
Penologist

Petroleum Researcher
Petroleum Geologist
Photojournalist
Political Scientist
Political Strategist
Project Engineer
Protozoologist
Quality Control Engineer
Quantitative Psychologist
Recording Engineer
Researcher, any subject
Right-of-Way Agent
Seismologist
Sociologist
Solicitor
Space Physicist
Statistician
Survey Worker
Systems Analyst
Tax Fraud Investigator
Writer

ENTREPRENEUR

'Super salesperson, entrepreneur'– these are words that describe you. The person who sold 'ice cubes to Eskimos' certainly belonged to your type. Your natural enthusiasm and ability to know what makes others tick and how to get them involved in your enterprises makes you one of the most charismatic and successful salespeople of all times.

You are a natural leader and cannot even imagine yourself taking orders from anyone! You are at your best in an occupation where you are totally your own boss or working as an independent contractor.

You have imagination, initiative, energy, confidence and are excellent at solving problems. You appear never to get tired and have enormous energy as long as your interest is high. However, this energy does run down, and when it does, your body may very well make you sick. That's the only time you will rest!

Your biggest problem is your dislike of routine and you tend to lose interest even in your own projects once all the problems are solved. Without quite a bit of self discipline, you may find you waste a lot of time and may even fail to complete all your projects.

You can be an inspiring teacher, writer, politician, actor, minister, salesperson, media personality, business entrepreneur, or anything else that interests you. Just get someone else to run the show once you have it off the ground.

Please avoid the military or any other 'establishment' type occupation where you have to obey someone else's rules and regulations. You must feel free to do what you have to do. 'I've Gotta Be Me' could well be your theme song.

DESCRIPTIVE WORDS: Influential, alert, creative, enthusiastic, independent, inspirational, optimistic, imaginative, intuitive, adaptable. Uncanny sense of knowing other's motivations, impulsive, charismatic.

Suggested Careers for ENFP's

Actor/Actress
Adventurer
Advertising Account
Executive
Anthropologist
Arbitrator
Archeologist
Artist's Agent
Astrologer
Audio-Visual Specialist
Barrister (Attorney)
Buyer
Clergy
Communications Consultant
Conciliator
Conference Interpreter
Consumer Services
Consultant
Drama Coach
Educator, any level, any subject
Educational Consultant
Educational Psychologist
Educational Therapist
Entrepreneur
Estate Agent (Real Estate
   Agent)
Employment Counsellor
Evangelist
Fashion Coordinator
Fashion Designer

Film, Radio, T.V. Actor,
   Director,
   Producer/Presenter
Foreign Correspondent
Fund Raiser
Interior Designer
Lobbyist
Marketing Director
Membership Solicitor
Museum Exhibit Designer
News Editor
News Reporter
Newspaper Columnist
Newspaper Editorial Writer
Passenger Service
Representative
Personal Manager
Photographer
Political Scientist
Politician (any level)
Political Strategist
Promoter
Psychologist
Psychiatrist
Public Relations Officer
Recreation Leader
Sales Manager
Travel Agent

TROUBLE SHOOTER

There's an old folk song about a 'gamblin man' and it may well have been about you. Not that you are necessarily a gambler, but you have the 'cool', an ability to be completely unemotional and quick thinking, skills necessary not only for a gambler, but also for an athlete, airplane pilot, diplomat, performer or any other occupation where it is the process more than the product that matters.

You good-naturedly accept whatever is going on. You really are able to live in the 'here and now' and let 'bygones be bygones'. You do not waste a lot of physical or emotional energy wishing things were not what they are. You don't look back with regret or forward with anticipation. When a situation or person no longer pleases you, you move on.

You may have an innate ability to handle tools, materials, or your own body, which can give you a mechanical, athletic or artistic gift. You will work at something you are interested in until it reaches the state of perfection that satisfies you. 'Practice makes perfect' may well be a slogan you live by.

You are tolerant, unprejudiced, open-minded and generally enjoy life. You may have a knack for analysing a situation, easing tensions and getting things moving again, certainly good qualities for a trouble-shooter or diplomat.

Some people may look upon you as unfeeling or aloof. It isn't that you don't care, but you can get so involved in your own projects that you sometimes forget to appreciate the other people around you. Your biggest problem, if you don't get interested in something important to you, is that you could become the proverbial 'rolling stone'.

Please avoid anything that smacks of scholarly research, or where you won't know the results for a long time! You want your reward to be immediate! You want to know you've won the game, completed the project, created the meal; waiting for 'pie in the sky' sometime in the future isn't your style at all!

DESCRIPTIVE WORDS: Resourceful, realistic, impulsive, friendly, suave, sophisticated, tolerant, mechanical, witty, clever, pragmatic, 'cool', courageous, unpredictable.

Suggested Careers for ESTP's

Actor
Adventurer
Airline Pilot
Air Traffic Controller
Airport Security Officer
Anaesthesiologist
Athlete
Athletic Trainer /Coach
Auctioneer
Auto/Motorcycle Racer
Building Contractor
Cinematographer
Clothes Designer
Commercial Artist
Commercial Photographer
Construction Engineer
Construction Estimator
Construction Superintendent
Construction Worker (any area)
Costume Designer
Customs Patrol Officer
Dancer
Deep Sea Diver
Detective
Dispatcher
Display Director
Electrician
Design Drafter
Emergency Medical Technician
Diplomat
Exploration Geophysicist
Engineering Surveyor
Fireman
Fire-Protection Engineer
Film Producer/Director

Flying Instructor
Forester
Foreign Correspondent
Gambler
Gynaecologist
Highway Contractor
Highway Inspector
Hydrographic Survey
Technician
Immigration Control Officer
    (Border Patrol Agent)
Industrial Engineering Tech.
Industrial X-Ray Operator
International Banker
Jockey
Labour Relations Consultant
Land Surveyor
Law Enforcement Officer
    (Policeman/woman)
Logging Contractor
Logistics Engineer
Marine Engineer
Mechanic
Machine Operator (any kind)
Medical Photographer
Marine Machinist
Marine Surveyor
Military Service
Mine Superintendent
Naval Architect
News Analyst
News Assistant
News Art Director
News Photographer
News Reporter

Nurse Anaesthetist
Ocean Engineer
Oceanographic Technician
Oil Field Pipeline Supervisor
Open Pit Mining Engineer
Petroleum Engineer
Photographic Engineer
Photojournalist
Purchasing Agent
Recording Engineer
Retail Store Art Director
Roulette Dealer
Set Designer
Special Effects Technician

Stage Manager
Stockbroker
Surgeon
Surgical Technologist
Surveyor
Tax Fraud Investigator
Technical Illustrator
TV Cameraman, Soundman
TV Director/Producer
Tool & Die Maker
Tool Designer
Yacht Designer
Yacht Racer

ESFP – EXTRAVERT, SENSATION, FEELING, PERCEPTIVE

LIFE OF THE PARTY

Easy-going, adaptable, optimistic, friendly, practical, non-judgemental, you are the oil that keeps the parts running smoothly. Because you can 'keep your cool', are aware of the needs of the moment, and have a tolerance for others, you are great working with people in crisis, or as a trouble shooter or on an athletic team. You also may be a great entertainer.

Your mind is like a file cabinet of information, and you can get to it instantly. You can remember where things are, who wants them, and why, without effort or lists. You probably have a good memory for stories, jokes, songs, and events, an ability that makes you a real social asset. You may also have a gift for being able to think on your feet, to ad-lib with great facility, an easy spontaneity, an ability that can be very valuable to an entertainer or any person where verbal facility is important.

Many ESFP's have an instinctive sense of design, for materials, line, colour, and texture, a talent important to artists and designers in all areas.

Your ability to remember enormous quantities of details, numbers, names, etc. can make you a very valuable salesperson.

Because you dislike feeling 'boxed in', be sure that your work enables you to get out and around fairly frequently, where you can use your charm to win friends and influence people – and get paid for it! If your interest lies in that direction you might make a great politician!

You need to be in a kind of work where the reward is immediate. You don't like to wait – you want the applause, the winners check, the finished product NOW!

Please avoid any kind of occupation that might be considered scholarly or one where you have to be by yourself a great deal of the time. You're best when you're around lots of other people and where the action is!

DESCRIPTIVE WORDS: Warm, attractive, optimistic, voluble, smooth, witty, charming, clever, open, generous, entertaining, sophisticated, sociable,impulsive, observant, spontaneous, uninhibited, adventuresome.

Suggested Careers for ESFP'S

Actor
Adventurer
Alternative Therapy Practitioner
Art Director
Athlete
Automobile Salesperson
Athletic Trainer/Coach
Airline Flight Attendant
Artist
Automobile Race Driver
Broadcasting Announcer
Buyer
Cartoonist
Caterer
Charity Aid Worker
Chiropodist
Cook, Chef
Consumer Financial Advisor
Creche Attendant (Nursery
    School Attendant)
Customer Service Rep.
Dance Therapist
Dentist
Dialysis Technician
Dietician
Directory Assistance Operator
Display Director
Elementary School Teacher
Emergency Medical
Technician
Entertainer
Estate Agent (Real Estate Agent)
Estate Manager
Exercise Physiologist
Explorer

Farmer, Farm Manager
Fashion Coordinator
Fashion Designer
Fashion Display Specialist
Film Producer/Director
Fire Chief
Fire Inspector
Fire Sprinkler Installer
Floral Designer
Flying Instructor
Food Broker
Food & Beverage Manager
Foreign Correspondent
Field Service Representative
Graphic Artist
Grain Broker
Gynaecologist
Hair Stylist/Barber
Health Club Attendant
Home Economist
Home Extension Agent
Hospital Admitting Clerk
Hotel Bell Captain
Hotel Manager
Industrial Arts Teacher
Information Clerk
Inhalation Therapist
Instructional Technologist
Interior Designer
Jeweller
Jockey
Labour Relations Consultant
Labour-Union Business Agent
Landscape Architect
Legal Assistant

Legal Secretary
Legislative Reporter
Letter Carrier
Lobbyist
Manual Arts Therapist
Masseur/Masseuse
Media Special Effects
Designer/Technician
Medical Office Receptionist
Medical Assistant
Medical Social Worker
Makeup Artist
Membership Solicitor
Midwife
Mobile Canteen Operator
Model
Modelling Instructor
Museum Exhibit Designer
Music Therapist
Naturopathic Physician
News Analyst
News Assistant
Newspaper Art Director
News Photographer
News Reporter
Nurse's Aide
Nursing Sister/Matron (Nurse,
   LVN Nurses's Aide)
Nutritionist
Office Nurse
Occupational Therapist
Optician
Ophthalmologist
Orientation & Mobility Therapist
Oral Surgeon/ Orthodontist
Passenger Service Representative
Pediatrician

Periodontist
Personal Assistant /Manager
Photographer
Photojournalist
P. E. Instructor
Physical Therapist
Pilot
Politician
Pollster
Professional Sports Competitor
Promotion Designer
Prosthetics Technician
Prosthetist
Psychiatric Nurse
Psychiatric Social Worker
Public Health Worker
Public Relations
Radiation Therapist
Range Manager
Receptionist
Recreation Leader
Recreational Therapist
Referral Aide
Reflexologist
Respiratory Therapist
Retail Sales Person
Sales Representative
Secretary
Set Designer
Social Director
Special Education Teacher
Speech Pathologist
Special Events Promoter
Stage Manager
Stock Broker
Survey Worker
Teacher's Aide

Teacher of the Handicapped
TV Film, Radio
Director/Producer
Textile Stylist
Theatre Arts Teacher
Tourist Information Assistant
Travel Agent

Travel Info Centre Supervisor
Veterinarian Surgeon (Vet)
Video Operator
Wardrobe Supervisor
Wedding Consultant
Yacht Racer

ORIGINAL THINKER

You are the scientists, researchers, scholars and inventors. (Dr. Jung himself was of your type.) You have a unique way of looking at the world and often express yourself well in writing. You can organise your ideas and express them clearly and succinctly. Your introverted nature enables you to work for long periods of time on whatever project you are focusing at the moment, and you dislike interruptions to your train of thought.

It is important for you to remember when and if you are organising people, that their feelings are important; a fact you are apt to overlook. You are probably one of whom it is said, "he doesn't suffer fools gladly" and you may appear to others to be cold, distant or aloof because of your objective, analytical approach to people, things and events.

In spite of this, you are a natural leader, especially in the way of ideas. Try not to let the occasional necessity of sociability and small talk bore you – even though you find it a terrible waste of time!

Don't allow anyone or anything to get you into a job that has too much routine and/or the necessity to remember and use lots of data or machines of any sort. It is important for you to keep your vision clear and let others handle the details – or the sales! Get a good secretary and let your computer do the data storage!

DESCRIPTIVE WORDS: Curious, self-confident, intuitive, theoretical, realistic, open-minded, unemotional, rational, methodical, careful, analytical.

Suggested Careers for INTJ's

Aeronautical Engineer
Archeologist
Architect
Aerospace Engineer
Agricultural Economist
Analytical Statistician
Anthropologist
Applied Mathematician
Applications Programmer
Astrologer
Astronomer
Bacteriologist
Barrister/Solicitor (Lawyer)
Biochemist
Biologist
Biostatistician
Botanist
Business Analyst
Business Consultant
Cardiologist
Chemical Oceanographer
Chemist
Chief Petroleum Engineer
City Planner
Computer Applications Engineer
Computer Programmer
Cryptanalyst
Cyberneticist
Cytologist
Data Processing System Analyst
Economic Analyst
Economist
Economic Geographer
Electromechanism Designer

Electronics Engineer
Engineering Technical Writer
Entologist
Environmental Scientist
Environmental Planner
Experimental Psychologist
Exploration Physicist
Financial Advisor
Financial Analyst
Forensic Pathologist
Forensic Toxicologist
Geneticist
Geological Engineer
Geo-microbiologist
Geomorphologist
Geophysicist
Geothermal Geologist
Health Physicist
Herpetologist
Histologist
Horticulturist
Ichthyologist
Industrial Economist
Industrial Editor
Industrial Engineer
Industrial Health Physicist
Industrial Microbiologist
Industrial Pharmacologist
Information Consultant
Information Processing Engineer
Information Scientist
Information System Programmer
Insurance Analyst
Insurance Sales Underwriter
Intelligent Research Specialist

International Lawyer
Internist
Invertebrate Paleontologist
Job Analyst
Judge
Marine Biologist
Marine Ecologist
Marine Geologist
Market Research Analyst
Marine Meteorologist
Material Scientist
Mathematician
Mathematical Statistician
Medical Physicist
Metallurgical Engineer
Meteorologist
Metrologist
Microbiologist
Mineralogist
Mineral Process Engineer
Mining Engineer
Mycologist
Naval Architect
Nematologist
Neurologist
Neuropharmacolgist
News Analyst
Newspaper Columnist
Newspaper Editorial Writer
Ocean Engineer

Oceanographer
Oceanographic Technician
Operation Research Analyst
Ornithologist
Otolaryngologist
Paleontologist
Parasitologist
Pathologist
Petroleum Geologist
Pharmacologist
Plastics Engineer
Physicist
Psychiatrist
Psychologist
Protozoologist
Political Scientist
Pollution Control Engineer
Production Planning
Supervisor
Space Physicist
Public Finance Specialist
Research mathematician
Seismologist
Statistician
Systems Analyst
Traffic Manager
Urban Sociologist
Writer

PSYCHIC

You have an almost uncanny ability to know what is going on with other people and often with animals, what could be called 'psychic'. Because of your highly developed intuitive faculty, you may sometimes feel misunderstood by people who do not understand your very insightful point of view. You do want to know that what you do 'matters' and makes life better or easier in some way for other people in society.

You definitely function best in a 'person-to-person' situation. You are an excellent interviewer, psychologist, counsellor, therapist or teacher, any position where you control the situation and do not have to deal with too many distractions. You have very distinct ideas of right and wrong and prefer to live within the established rules. You like to have your life organised and not too much left to chance.

Although you are able to handle people with sympathy and understanding, you prefer not to be placed in an executive position unless you can delegate someone else to take care of the details and do the 'dirty work'. You prefer to be the power behind the throne, so to speak.

Intuitives lose interest in any job once they have found out how to do it, so it is best that whatever position you find yourself in has variety and is a challenge to your highly original and creative mind. You will definitely want to avoid any kind of situation where you are not working with people of integrity and honesty as you do not work well in a critical, hostile atmosphere.

DESCRIPTIVE WORDS: Psychic, mystic, poetic, reserved, organised, decisive, sensitive, scholarly, insightful, creative, innovative, complex, sincere, personally warm, leader behind the scenes.

Suggested Careers for INFJ's

Actor/Actress
Archeologist
Architect
Alternative Therapy Practitioner
Animal Trainer
Anthropologist
Art Therapist
Astrologer
Book Editor
Casework Supervisor
Charity Worker
Child Psychologist
Clergy
Clinical Psychologist
College Planning &
   Placement Counsellor
Costume Specialist
Counsellor
Criminologist
Dancer/
   Therapist/Choreographer
Ecologist
Employee Welfare Manager
Environmentalist
Educational Consultant
Employment Interviewer
Employment Counsellor
Financial Aid Counsellor
Fashion Writer /Designer
Foreign Student Adviser
Guidance Counsellor
Group Leader (Social Service)
Geriatric Social Worker
Hospital Personnel Director
Hypnotherapist

Industrial Sociologist
Industrial Occupational Analyst
Job Analyst
Manual Arts Therapist
Marine Biologist
Marine Ecologist
Marine Geologist
Marine Meteorologist
Market Research Analyst
Medical Office Receptionist
General Practioner Medical
Medical Parasitologist
Medical Physicist
Meteorologist
Microbiologist
Medical Technologist
Mental Health Technician
Modelling Instructor
Museum Curator
Museum Exhibit Designer
Music Therapist
Mycologist
Nematologist
Neurologist
Neuropharmacologist
News Analyst
News Assistant
Newspaper Columnist
News Editorial Writer
News Reporter
Nursing Home Recreational
   Therapist
Nursing Home Social Worker
Nutritionist
Oceanographer

Oceanographic Technician
Ornithologist
Naturopathic Physician
Occupational Therapist
Orientation & Mobility
Therapist
Paleontologist
Pathologist
Personnel Director
Penologist
Poet//Dramatist/Novelist
Political Scientist
Pollution Control Engineer

Physician (Internist)
Physical Therapist
Physiologist
Protozoologist
Psychic
Psychologist
Psychiatrist
Social Worker
Solicitor
Toxicologist
Urban Sociologist
Veterinarian Surgeon (Vet)

RECORDER

Because of your introverted nature, you are able to work by yourself for considerable periods of time, preferably with few distractions. Your mind acts somewhat like a computer, and can remember quantities of facts and figures and pull them from your memory bank whenever necessary. You also have a great deal of common sense and like to keep life and events based on facts and not too fanciful. Since you are objective, analytical, logical, critical, and like having a system and structure within which to work, you seem to function better with machines and numbers rather than people. You are excellent at maintaining and keeping an operation functioning when your objective, analytical nature can be used profitably. You may very well be able to work efficiently and effectively with your hands.

You like to know what is expected of you, and when, and don't mind working to deadlines. Too many loose ends or open-ended situations make you feel uneasy. However, you may find you sometimes jump to conclusions too hastily. Remember to get all the information necessary before coming to a decision.

You will do your best in a field where your ability to remember details, analyse what went wrong, and get things organised is important.

Fancy speech, dress, manners or surroundings are relatively unimportant to you, and you are probably most comfortable in a situation where they are not essential.

DESCRIPTIVE WORDS: Analytical, dependable, cautious, conservative, thorough, dutiful, practical, sensible, neat, orderly, obedient and steady.

Suggested Careers for ISTJ's

Athlete, Professional
Abstractor
Accountant (C.P.A)
Accounting Clerk
Accounting Systems Expert
Acupuncturist
Aerial Photographer Interpreter
Aerospace Librarian
Airline Pilot
Air Traffic Controller
Agricultural Commodity Grader
Apartment Building Super.
Assembler, Production Line
Audiological Technician
Auditor
Banker/any position/department
Bio-medical Engineer
Bond Analyst
Bookkeeper
Brokerage Clerk
Budget Officer
Building Inspector
Business Analyst
Charge Account Clerk
Check Processing Clerk
Chemist
Claims Adjuster
Collections Clerk
Collections Manager
Comptroller
Computer Programmer
Computer Operator
Construction Industry–
　Any position:
　Estimator,

Inspector,
Superintendent,
Carpenter,
Painter,
Electrician,
Plumber etc.
Credit Analyst
Court Reporter
Criminologist
Data Base Manager
Documents Examiner
Electrical Inspector
Electrical Equipment Repairs
Electronic Communication
Technician
Embalmer
Engineer
Dermatologist
Dispensing Optician
Estate Appraiser
Estimator
Export Clerk
Fiber Technologist
File Clerk
Film Librarian
Finance Company Manager
Financial Statement Clerk
Fingerprint Classifier
Fire Inspector Forensic Expert
Foreign Exchange Clerk
Fruit & Vegetable Grader
Gemologist
Geologist
Glass Inspector
Grain Manager

Harbour Master
Heating Plant Superintendent
Medical Technologist
Insurance Claims Examiner
Insurance Clerk
Law Enforcement Officer
Legal Assistant
Legal Secretary
Legislative Reporter
Loan Officer
Machine Operator any kind
Mail Clerk
Mail Room Supervisor
Maintenance Data Analyst
Manifest Clerk
Mechanic
Mechanical Inspector
Media Clerk
Medical Librarian
Medical Records Clerk
Medical Voucher Clerk
Metallurgist
Meteorologist
Meter Inspector
Microfilm Technologist
Micrographics Services Super.
Mineral Processing Engineer
Mining Engineer
Occupational Safety & Health
    Inspector
Ophthalmic Lens Inspector

Optician
Order Detailer
Parts & Order Stock Clerk
Pawnbroker
Payroll Clerk
Petroleum Engineer
Petroleum Inspector
Pharmacist
Proofreader
Pulp & Paper Tester
Purchasing Agent
Quantity Surveyor
Securities Analyst
Solicitor
Stationary Engineer
Statistician
Stockroom Supervisor
Systems Analyst
Tax Accountant
Traffic Rate Clerk
Trust Evaluation Clerk
TV Cameraman,Soundman
Ultra-Sound Technologist
Warehouse Manager
Water Treatment-Plant
Operator
Weight Engineer

MAN FRIDAY

Whatever you do, you want to be sure it is going to help make someone happy, rich or more comfortable. For you, pleasing people is very important. If someone were sick and needed lots of tender loving care, you're the one to be called. Not only would you be concerned about their physical needs and their emotional state, but you would also remember their medicines, the time they are to be given, who had sent cards, who had been to visit, what the doctor had said, and any other information that you had heard, seen or read. Your ability to remember many details is truly remarkable.

You are also able to be alone and to concentrate for long periods of time, qualities needed by anesthesiologists, secretaries, nurses, librarians, therapists or other fields where working concentratedly with only a few people is important.

You will never break the rules, because you prefer to work in an established and expected manner. You are totally dedicated to a person or an institution and will take on extra work rather than feel that something won't be done properly. In fact, that may be your greatest weakness – that you do all the work yourself!

DESCRIPTIVE WORDS: Caring, conscientious, conventional, dedicated, nurturing, traditional, dependable, practical, loyal, devoted, kind, friendly, hard working.

Suggested Careers for ISFJ's

Acupuncturist
Alternative Therapy Practitioner
Airline Passenger Attendant
Air Traffic Controller
Anaesthesiologist
Anaesthetist
Archivist
Art Conservator
Art Librarian
Bank Secretary
Biological Science Librarian
Buyer
Career Information Specialist
Chemical Librarian
Chef
Child Care Supervisor
Child Development Associate
Chiropractor
Child Psychologist
College Registrar
Communications Librarian
Community Nurse
Community Pharmacist
Conservationist
Court Reporter
Creche Attendant (Nursery School)
Dental Assistant
Dental Hygienist
Dentist
Dermatologist
Designer
Dietician
Educational Therapist

Endodontist
Educational Attendance Clerk
Educational Audio-Visual Spec.
Environmentalist
Environmental Scientist
Executive Secretary
Exercise Physiologist
Farm Management Advisor
Farmer
File Clerk
Film Librarian
Financial Aid Counsellor
Floriculturist
Forest Nursery Supervisor
Forest Ranger
Forest Technician
Game Warden
Gardener
General Practice Doctor
Geriatric Nurse
Geriatric Physical Therapist
Geriatric Psychologist
Geriatric Social Worker
Graphic Artist
Groundskeeper
Health Science Librarian
Hair Stylist
Historian
Home Economist
Hospital Admitting Clerk
Information Manager
Inhalation Therapist
Insurance Clerk
Journal Clerk
Laboratory Assistant

Legal Assistant
Legal Secretary
Legal Stenographer
Legislative Reporter
Lens Prescription Clerk
Librarian
Library Technical Assistant
Loan Interviewer
Makeup Artist
Manual Arts Therapist
Marriage & Family Counsellor
Masseur
Media Clerk
Medical Assistant
Medical Librarian
Medical Office Receptionist
Medical Records Clerk
Medical Secretary
Midwife
Mobile Canteen Operator
Museum Curator
Music Librarian
News Assistant
Nurse's Aide
Nurse
Nutritionist
Occupational Therapist
Office Manager
Office Clerk
Optician
Optometric Assistant
Optometrist
Order Clerk
Orthodontist
Osteopathic Physician
Patient's Librarian
Pediatrician

Periodontist
Personal Assistant
Personnel Scheduler
Pharmacist
Photographer
Physical Education Instructor
Private Secretary
Psychiatrist
Psychologist
Physical Therapist
Podiatrist
Preservationist
Primary School Teacher
Prosthetist
Public Health Worker
Public Health Nurse
Radiation Therapist
Receptionist
Recreational Therapist
Referral Aide
Reservation Clerk
Respiratory Therapist
Secretary
Special Education Teacher
Speech Pathologist
Social Worker
Surgical Technologist
Stage Manager
Teacher's Aide
Teacher of the Handicapped
Travel Agent
Urologist
Veterinarian
Wedding Consultant
Wardrobe Supervisor

PHILOSOPHER

You really want to say it right. Sometimes in your zeal to express yourself fully and exactly, you confuse others whose minds cannot reach the subtleties yours can. The great philosophers of the world must have been **INTP's**, because yours is the type of mind that is interested in what makes the world and the objects in it tick! You love analysing and organising facts and ideas and are good at it. But try to avoid dealing with 'people problems' unless it is absolutely unavoidable.

Not only are you extremely accurate in your use of language, but you are also fascinated with it and may find yourself concentrating on a particular meaning or the right way of saying something for long periods of time. In fact, you may even forget to eat when you get really involved in whatever your current project is, which could very easily be writing a book.

You may appear to others to be arrogant, insensitive and intolerant. But only to those whose minds are slower to comprehend than yours. You can be very impatient with what seems to you stupidity or unnecessary routine. Patience is a virtue you may want to develop.

You make excellent professors, researchers, scholars, philosophers, mathematicians, scientists or psychologists. Please avoid anything that smacks of materialism or commercialism. Leave the sales to others. You create the ideas, the theories and the philosophies.

DESCRIPTIVE WORDS: Precise, accurate, logical, coherent, curious, intelligent, scholarly, persevering, independent, analytical.

Suggested Careers for ITNP's

Agricultural Chemist	Economic Analyst
Agricultural Entomologist	Ecology Ranger
Agricultural Microbiologist	Engineer
Agronomist	Engineering Technical Writer
Analytical Chemist	Engineering Technician
Anatomist	Environmental Engineer
Anthropologist	Environmental Planner
Aquatic Biologist	Exploration Geophysicist
Arboretum Researcher	Experimental Psychologist
Archeologist	Financial Analyst
Architect	Forensic Pathologist
Art Historian	Food Scientist
Astronomer	Forest Ecologist
Astrologer	Forensic Specialist
Audiologist	Geodesist
Botanist	Geneticist
Biologist	Geographer
Chemist	Geological Engineer
Chemical Engineer	Geologist
City Planner	Geo-Microbiologist
Computer Programmer	Geomorphologist
Computer Technician	Geophysicist
Computational Linguist	Geothermal Geologist
Criminologist	Highway Engineer
Cryptographer	Histologist
Cyberneticist	Horticulturist
Cytologist	Ichthyologist
Cytotechnician	Industrial Designer
Cytotecynologist	Industrial Health Physicist
Design Engineer	Industrial Engineer
Display Director	Industrial Pharmacologist
Drafting Technician	Industrial Microbiologist
Earth Scientist	Information System Programmer
Ecologist	Information Scientist
Economist	Lexicographer

Management Analyst
Market Research Analyst
Marine Ecologist
Marine Biologist
Marine Meteorologist
Marine Geologist
Mathematician
Mathematical Statistician
Mechanical Design Engineer
Medical Research
Medical Parasitologist
Medical Physicist
Metallurgist
Meteorologist
Microbiologist
Mineralogist
Mycologist
Nematologist
Neurologist
Neuropharmacologist
Novelist
Nuclear Engineer
Nuclear Physicist
News Analyst/Editorial Writer
Oceanographer
Operational Research Analyst
Optician
Ophthalmologist
Ornithologist
Paleontologist
Parasitologist
Pathologist
Penologist
Petrologist

Pharmacologist
Physicist
Physiologist
Plastics Engineer
Pollution Control Engineer
Political Analyst
Political Scientist
Polygraph Examiner
Private Detective
Production Engineer
Protozoologist
Psychoanalyst
Psychiatrist
Quantitative Psychologist
Quality Control Engineer
Quality Control Technician
Rate & Cost Analyst
Reporter
Research Mathematician
Secret Service Personnel
Safety Engineer
Solicitor
Seismologist
Soil Scientist
Space Physicist
Statistician
Systems Analyst
Tax Fraud Investigator
Technical Writer
Theologist
Toxicologist
Traffic Manager
Urban Sociologist

MISSIONARY

On the surface you may appear quite reserved, but when someone gets to know you well, they find you have a warm, deeply caring side, especially regarding something or someone important to you.

It is very important to you that what you do 'matters', that your work contributes in some positive way to the betterment of society, through improved human understanding, health or happiness. You have to know your work has value beyond the pay cheque you receive.

You are very sensitive and may be vulnerable to the opinions of others who do not value what you value. This can give you a sense of inferiority which is not justified.

It is important that you work in a place or field where you may express your ideals and convictions. This may be in the ministry, teaching, psychology, art, acting or in an institution or charity dedicated to the care of people or through writing. You could also be a good psychic!

You will want to avoid any commercial profession such as banking, business or accounting. People matter much more than money to you.

DESCRIPTIVE WORDS: Reticent, shy, calm, deeply caring, idealistic, sacrificial, committed to what is positive, good, beautiful, moral, adaptable, patient with complicated situations, harmonious, sensitive, aware, courteous.

Suggested Careers for INFP's

Actor/Actress
Advertising
Airline Passenger Attendant
Alternative Therapies
Practitioner
Architect
Art Director
Astrologer
Charity Worker
Clergy
Clinical Psychologist
College Planning & Placement
Conference Interpreter
Counsellor
Criminologist
Creche Attendant
Dance Therapist
Designer
Ecologist
Educational Therapist
Employment Counsellor
Educational Psychologist
Environmentalist
Estate Agent (Residential)
Foreign Student Advisor
Geriatric Psychologist
Geriatric Social Worker
Guidance Counsellor
Health Officer
Hospital Admitting Clerk
Hospital Personnel Director
Hypnotherapist
Employment Interviewer
Industrial Sociologist
Inhalation Therapist

Interior Designer
Internist
Interviewer
Labour Relations Consultant
Literary Agent
Makeup Artist
Manual Arts Therapist
Masseuse
Missionary
Naturopathic Physician
Music Therapist
Neurologist
Newspaper Columnist
News Editorial Writer
Recreational Therapist
Religious Institution/ any
    position
Nursing Home Worker
Nutritionist
Occupational Therapist
Passenger Service Representative
Penologist
Personal Assistant
Prisoner Classification
Political Scientist
Primary School Teacher
Probation Officer
Psychiatrist
Psychologist
Public Health Educator/Worker
Receptionist
Recreation Leader
Recreational Therapist
Religious Activities Director
Retirement Officer

Secretary
Social Worker
Social Psychologist
Sociologist
Special Education Teacher

Teacher of the Handicapped
Theatre Arts Teacher
Urban Sociologist
Veterinarian

ISTP – INTROVERT, SENSATION, **THINKING**, PERCEPTIVE

PERFORMER

You are the performers, the actors, the artisans, the athletes. Whatever you do, you are more concerned with the process than the product – unless the product is a flawless performance! You are willing to expend considerable amounts of time and energy working to perfect a skill or a piece of art. You will work until whatever it is, is as PERFECT as you can make it, but only if YOU want to do it! You have probably not been the teacher's pet in school! You like best working with the tangibles of the world. You may handle tools with great facility and may become proficient in any field where that ability is useful, such as mechanics. Or you may consider your body a tool and tune it so it will perform to your command!

If your interests are not technical, mechanical, or athletic, you may use your mind to help you analyse systems or markets. You may enjoy taking a confused bunch of figures or materials and create order out of the chaos. Whatever you do, it will have to make 'sense'.

You prefer to work alone and dislike interruptions. You don't enjoy being in a situation where you have to please a lot of people, unless of course those people are observing you from the grandstand! Then you are at your best – using your ability to react, think quickly and adapt to the needs of the moment. This same ability may make you a good professional athlete, a trouble shooter, a surgeon, any occupation where you can use your quick thinking and ability to live in the moment. No doubt, Ian Fleming had your type in mind when he created James Bond!

Please avoid any routine employment such as clerical work, and try to cultivate completing one task before taking on another.

DESCRIPTIVE WORDS: Energetic, action-oriented, factual, practical, loner, perfectionist, disciplined, concentrated, realistic,

Suggested Careers for ISTP's

Accountant
Anaesthesiologist
Acoustics Engineer
Airline Pilot
Air Traffic Controller
Appliance Installer/Repairer
Architect
Athlete, Professional,
   Competitor
Athletic Coach/Manager
Audio Technician
Aviation Technician
Book Designer
Bookkeeper
Bricklayer
Cabinet Maker
Calibrator
Carpenter
Carpet Installer
Cartographer
Cartoonist
Ceramic Design Engineer
Chef/Cook
Chemical Lab Technician
Cinematographer
Clothes Designer
Commercial Artist
Commercial Photographer
Computer Programmer
Computer Systems Service
   Technician
Construction Industry–any
   role, any equipment, any level
Costume Designer
Cytotechnologist

Dancer
Dental Ceramicist
Dispensing Optician
Display Director
Deep Sea Diver
Draftsman
Drafting Technician
Electrical Control Assembler
Electromyographic Technician
Elevator Constructor
Electroplater
Electrotyper
Engineer
Environmental Health
Technician
Farm Mechanic
Fashion Designer
Fashion Display Specialist
Film Editor/Producer
Film Lab Technician
Fireman
Fire Sprinkler Installer
Fishery Engineer
Fishery Technician
Foreign Correspondent
Football Coach
Forms Analyst & Designer
Goldsmith
Graphic Artist/Designer
Heating & Air-Conditioning
Technician
Hydraulic Engineer
Hydrographic Survey
Technician
Illuminating Engineer

Industrial Engineer Technician	Nuclear Medical Technologist
Industrial X-Ray Operator	Oceanographer/Technician
Irrigation Engineer	Oil Field Pipeline Supervisor
Jeweller	Open Pit Mining Engineer
Journalist	Opththmologist
Lab-Test Mechanic	Optician
Landscape Architect	Optometrist
Land Surveyor	Oral Pathologist
Laser Technician	Oral Surgeon
Law Enforcement Personnel	Orthodontic Technician
Lens Grinder	Orthodontist
Letter Carrier	Package Designer
Lithographer	Periodontist
Marine Engineer	Performer
Marine Machinist	Petroleum Engineer
Marine Surveyor	Photographic Engineer
Mechanic - any kind, any machine	Photographic Equipment Tech.
Medical Chemistry Technologist	Photojournalist
Medical Illustrator	Photolithographer
Medical Photographer	Plastic Surgeon
Memorial Designer	Plumber
Metallographer	Polygraph Examiner
Metallurgical Engineer & Tech.	Promotion Designer
Meteorologist	Prosthetics Technician
Meter Inspector	Prosthetist
Microfilm Technologist	Quality Control Technician
Military Services	Recording Engineer
Model Maker	Roulette Dealer
Motion Picture Projectionist	Safety Engineer
Museum Exhibit Designer	Safety Inspector
Musician	Security Analyst
Music Mixer	Set Designer
Naval Architect	Shopping Investigator
Neurosurgeon	Spectographer
Newspaper Art Director	Statistician
Newspaper Editor	Stationary Engineer
News Photographer	Surgeon

Surgical Technologist	Designer/technician
Surveyor	Tool & Die Maker
Systems Analyst	Topographic Surveyor
Technical Illustrator	Truck Driver
Tax Accountant/auditor	TV Camera operator
Tax Solicitor	Weight Engineer
Textile Stylist	Weapons Instrument Mechanic
Theatrical Special Effects	Yacht Designer/Racer

NATURALIST

'Back to nature' is a phrase that appeals to you, and you really know what it means when they say 'stop and smell the roses'. You love all that is simple, unaffected, and natural. You are happiest when you can work in an environment with animals and/or plants and apart from any 'establishment' type occupation.

You may have a bit of difficulty in expressing your feelings verbally and find your best means of expression through some kind of art or craft where you can put into visible form your intense, subjective and personal sensations and feelings for the outer world.

You will devote yourself totally to a job or to a person when you feel what you do is contributing in some way to the betterment of life on this earth. When you find yourself in such meaningful work, you may become so totally involved in it that you forget what time of day it is or even how long you have been working. You are willing to work at something until as the saying goes, 'Practice makes perfect'. This stick-to-it-iveness could make you a champion athlete or performer of some kind.

Try to avoid any occupation where you have to live by the rules set up by some one else or where there are a lot of 'have to's' and 'shoulds'. You would eventually rebel, so it is better if you can start out doing your 'own thing' in the world of nature that you love.

DESCRIPTIVE WORDS: Free-spirited, sensuous, warm, alive, original, creative, natural, fiercely independent, anti-establishment, accepting, kind, caring, nurturing, unprejudiced.

Suggested Careers for ISFP's

Acupuncturist	Fashion Designer
Actor	Floriculturist
Adventurer	Flying Instructor
Airline Passenger Services	Foreign Correspondent
Alternative Therapy Practitioner	Forest Nursery Supervisor
Anaesthetist	Furniture Designer/Maker
Animator	Game Warden
Artist	Garden Centre
Architect	Designer/Manager
Archeologist	Gardener
Athlete/ Professional Competitor	Goldsmith
Cabinet Maker	Graphic Artist
Cartoonist	Grounds keeper
Carpenter	Hairstylist
Barber	Horse Trainer
Botanist	Horticulturist
Braille Coder	Jeweller/ Jewellry Designer
Coach – Performing or Athletic	Jockey
Chiropractor	Journalist
Cook/Chef	Make-up Artist
Conservationist	Medical Illustrator
Creche Attendant	Model Maker
Costume Designer	Musician
Counsellor	Music Therapist
Dairy Farmer	Midwife
Dancer	Nutritionist
Dance Therapist	Nurse
Dentist	Occupational Therapist
Dental Hygienist	Orthodontist
Dermatologist	Osteopath
Designer	Periodontist
Dietician	Photographer
Ecologist	Potter
Environmentalist	Psychiatric Nurse
Farmer	Recreational Therapist

Respiratory Therapist
Sculptor
Special Effects Technician
Speech Therapist/Pathologist
Teacher of the Handicapped
Teacher-Primary School/
    Private Tutor

Theatre Arts/ any media/any job
Truck Driver
Travel Agent
Tool & Die Maker
Veterinarian
Wildlife Control Agent
Zoologist

Now that you know your type you may ask, "So what?" The next three chapters are addressed to students, job seekers and employers. But there may be those of you who have taken the PREFERENTIAL QUESTIONNAIRE in order to know yourself better and to understand how to get along with others. There are a few general observations I would like to make regarding how the knowledge of 'type' can help in human relationships.

First, the old adage, 'birds of a feather flock together', is definitely true when it comes to friendships with persons of the same sex, especially when it comes to the functions. Intuitives like intuitives, sensation types enjoy the company of fellow sensation types. Feeling types can be hurt by what appears to them to be a thinking type's coldness and conversely, a thinking type may well say 'sentimental garbage' to a feeling type's current enthusiasm. Introverts and extraverts can be great friends, as the introvert appreciates the extravert's ability to break the ice in social occasions.

But it is just the opposite when it comes to picking a mate. Then 'opposites attract' seems to be true. It is certainly one reason why what was initially a strong attraction and great 'love' can become aversion, a strong dislike or even hate.

In my years of observing how 'type' differences function in marriage, I have known many introverts who married extraverts, only to have them both complaining later. Extraverts want to go out, to be doing something, introverts want to stay home. and read a book. Sensation types marry intuitives with similar results. Sensation types love to shop and accumulate things; intuitives are bored to tears with shopping and 'things' don't interest them at all. Judging types marry perceptives. Judging types want to 'be on time', perceptives are always late! It is not difficult to understand why marriages where opposite types have joined together so often fail.

It can work, however, if instead of criticising and trying to change the other, each partner allows the other one to be true to who he/she is. It is well known that no one can change another person. But if you can try to understand your differences, they can be a positive rather than a negative factor in your relationship. Or, at least, you will understand that the other person is not against you, they are just being who they are! If you can appreciate each other's point of view, the differences can work FOR rather than AGAINST the relationship.

I have observed, however, that if you are friends first, and have at least one function you share - your chances of having a successful long-time relationship increase remarkably.

Within a family a knowledge of type can be most helpful. Fathers frequently expect their sons to be just like them and when they aren't there is unpleasantness and friction. There are brothers or sisters in a family who are so different from each other that the parents criticise and blame, praising one and not the other because they don't understand that each child is acting true to him or her-self, but not necessarily the way the parents expect. An intuitive child's room will probably be messy, and he or she will probably not remember where anything is; a sensation child's room will probably be orderly and he or she will remember everything! An intuitive child may be a better student, a sensation type a better athlete. A perceptive type child will act impulsively; a judgement type plans his or her activities; judgement types gets their homework done without prompting, perceptives may leave it to the last minute or not do it at all! A feeling type child will be affectionate, helpful and sympathetic; a thinking type child might be thought to be 'cold', critical and uncaring. An extraverted child will probably get along well at school and with his/her peer group; an introverted child may be described by a teacher as 'not participating'.

It has been observed that extraversion and introversion are inborn. Whether the functions are learned behaviour or inborn is still open to question.

A parent will get along best with a child who is of similar 'type' and have difficulty understanding one who is of an opposite type. But, hopefully, if parents can understand that their children are acting true to themselves and that their child or children are not being deliberately 'bad' or 'naughty' or 'unkind' and need to be appreciated and enjoyed for who they are, hopefully there will be more happy families and children.

There comes a time in every person's school life when choices need to be made. This is usually the time when one decides whether to emphasise the humanities or the sciences in continuing education. As much of school is directed to eventually earning a living, would it not be wise to take one's 'type' into consideration when deciding what subjects to take?

The 'mental discipline' of taking subjects which one finds difficult might be beneficial if discipline is what you're after, but if you are thinking towards a relatively stress-free future occupation, containing as little tension as possible, then it may be wise to select those subjects that one enjoys and where a good grade comes most easily.

The academic life will always be more amenable for those of you who are '**J**'s' because you are willing to work toward a goal and wait a bit for your reward. For you '**P's**' school may be difficult, as you want your reward immediately. You want to win the game, finish the painting, get the car to work, fix what has gone wrong, and you don't want to have to wait until the end of the term to know the result. It is important you direct your effort towards a career in which you will get your satisfaction or reward immediately and direct your academic studies accordingly. Physical Education, competitive sports, chemistry, where the result of an experiment is immediate, any of these could be a wise choice for you.

Intuitive feeling types will be more interested in history, literature, philosophy, psychology, people oriented fields. Intuitive thinkers will probably want to direct their academic choices towards science, mathematics, subjects leading to research, in any area. Sensation types will want to learn how to DO something practical, feeling types with people, thinking types with things!

Please, never mind what anybody says about "More money to be made in......" If it isn't compatible with you ARE, any money you make will be earned at the cost of your peace of mind. It has been my observation after twenty five years of observing how type influences careers, that when a person earns a living using his/her *primary* function, they LOVE what they are doing, and make money too! That is what I call SUCCESS!

The question often arises in an interview, "Why should we hire you?" or "How do you see yourself in this position?" It can be helpful in answering this kind of question to know some of the adjectives that describe one's type.

For example; if you are an extravert (**E**) and are applying for a selling job, a good response to the question would be something like this:

"I can see myself in this position because I am an outgoing person and can handle distractions without getting upset, or confused. I don't mind travelling. I enjoy meeting new people and experiencing new situations." All of these qualities are true for extraverts.

What about introverts (**I**)? How about this: "I realise that this job will keep me pretty isolated from my fellow workers. That is just fine with me. I prefer working by myself. In fact, just give me the job, shut the door, and I'll have it done in no time. I like to be by myself. I can concentrate for long periods of time and can say without risk of argument that I often get so involved in what I'm doing that I lose track of time."

For 'thinking' (**T**) types: You're logical, analytical, realistic, unemotional, objective and have the ability to organise people and things. You aren't sentimental or liable to be swayed by anything other than logical, realistic requests or arguments. "Boss par excellence".

For 'feeling' (**F**) types: You're kind, tactful, courteous, helpful, co-operative, appreciative, sympathetic, understanding, diplomatic. You are usually able to say and do the 'right' thing. You're the oil that can keep the parts running smoothly.

For 'sensation' (**S**) types: You're factual, realistic, with a good deal of common sense, a good memory, your 'feet are on the ground'. You prefer the familiar and expected ways of doing things and like a definite routine.

For 'intuitive' (**N**) types: You're imaginative, creative, spontaneous, original, willing to take risks, to try something new, interested in ideas and possibilities, good at solving problems. You don't like routine and will always be the one to seek new horizons, invent new things and find new and different ways of doing anything and everything!

If you're a 'judgement' (**J**) type you will see that whatever you have to do is completed on time and according to the standards set. You will be punctual and reliable, a person who can always be depended upon.

If you're 'perceptive'(**P**), you have flexibility, spontaneity, are easy-going, casual, patient with others and undemanding.

When you are looking for a job, the page you probably turn to most often is the APPOINTMENTS (Help Wanted) section of the newspaper. So the next question is- "How to know where to look?" To read every ad is time consuming, so look under the sections most apt to have the kind of job for which you are looking and will match your personality.

'SALES & MARKETING'

To do any kind of selling, one should be an (**E**). Extraverts enjoy meeting people, dealing with unknown and unfamiliar situations, and have the kind of energy needed to initiate activity, a necessary quality in every kind of selling. The one exception to this rule would be working behind a counter in a store. There, an introvert could be content. But if the selling takes any sort of initiative on the part of the salesperson extraversion is necessary.

If the job entails explaining complicated machinery or computer programmes or technology then it would be well to have developed (**S**) or (**T**) or both! If making friends with your customers is important, however, then be sure you are a (**F**) type person.

Marketing usually entails creating new ideas, opening new markets etc.; for that you should be an EXTRAVERT INTUITIVE!

'BUILDING & CONSTRUCTION'

For these jobs, The SENSATION (**S**) function needs to be the primary function. Introvert, extravert, thinking, feeling, all OK. But no intuitive should ever get into the building trade!

'HEALTH SERVICES'

These are jobs that are (or should be) patient oriented! Any work that focuses on caring for people needs an individual with the FEELING (**F**) function primary.

'HOTEL & CATERING'

Food preparation – SENSATION
Front desk skills – FEELING
Bookeeping – INTROVERT SENSATION THINKING

Almost every type can be used at some level if this is a field in which you see yourself.

'FILM & TELEVISION'

The field is so wide ranging, there is a place in it for every type.
Casting Director – INTUITION
Sets – SENSATION
Direction – FEELING INTUITIVE
Acting – INTROVERT INTUITIVE
Camera – SENSATION THINKING
Properties – SENSATION
Sound Technician – SENSATION THINKING
Programming – FEELING etc.

'ENGINEERING'

THINKING for every kind of engineering – even 'sales engineer' – what is needed in sales engineering is logical planning ability.

———

Now what about those ads that seem to want a person who has everything? It is important that they are read very carefully. Underline the key words. Let me give you a few examples from a recent *Daily Telegraph*.

"*The company seeks a <u>manager</u>* (**E**) *to head the <u>technical</u>* (**S,T**) *centre. The role will be very wide ranging.* (**E**).....*a senior member of the management team will be involved in ALL aspects of <u>product development</u>* (**N**) *and major <u>customer liaison</u>* (**E,F**).... *required to <u>attend conferences</u>,* (**E**) *<u>write technical papers</u>* (**T**) *and* *liaise* (**E**) *with other production facilities ......The position will be extremely challenging* (**N**), *requiring the individual to display first rate technical competence* (**T**,**S**) *over a range of technologies, interpersonal skills* (**F**) *and general business flair* (**N**)".

As we look at this advertisement it seems they want someone who is good at everything! But if we analyse it closely we see that EXTRAVERSION, INTUITION and THINKING are the most frequent qualities desired.

Intuitives and extraverts can generally get along with people (interpersonal skills) especially if they are in a management position and getting along with others is part of the job! This particular position requires travelling, something which extraverts usually enjoy. And a 'challenge' always appeals to intuitives. This kind of position could be right for you if you are an ENTJ or ENTP. Only extraverts enjoy going to conferences. Introverts will go but reluctantly!

Now let's read another:
"*....build and lead team (E) of design and development* (**N**) *engineers* (**T**), *....responsibility for production development from concept to production.* (**J**) (finish what is begun!)....
To complement your technical expertise (**S**,**T**) *you will be an expert communicator,* (**E**,**N**)*a 'networker'* (**E**) *of people with diverse skills, a project manager* (**E**,**T**) *and excellent presenter* (**E**) *of plans and concepts* (**E**).....(ENTJ or ESTJ).
In this job you would be working with engineers, who probably are thinking types, so you'd get along best if you are a thinking type also.

CORPORATE ACCOUNT MANAGER
"*....dual role requiring proven account development skills* (**F**,**N**) *manage small sales team* (**E**,**F**)*....applicants must have high level of intellect plus...flexibility.* (**P**) *and professionalism, significant travel* (**P**)
If you are an ENFP this might be a job for you!

PRODUCTION MANAGER (newspaper business)
"....objective is to improve the _planning, (**T**)control (**J**)and efficiency_
(**T**) of _production_ (**S**) operation" ..._technical_ (**S**) competence,
organisational ability (**T**) _computer literacy_ (**TS**).
This is a position for those with developed Sensation Thinking
functions - ISTJ's or ESTJ's.

GROUP AD MANAGER
Challenge (**N**) oriented, strong business acumen,..... required to
manage (**E**), _motivate,_ (**F,N**) and _develop sales_ (**E,N**) staff
within a tough, target driven (**J**) environment.... _Develop sales_
strategy (**E,F,N**) and _maintain budgetary control._ (**J**).._Team player,_
(**E**) _initiative,_ (**N**) _creativity_ (**N**), capacity to _communicate_ well at
all levels, (**E,F**), ability to _develop leads_ and '_make things_
happen'. (**E,N**).

Here's a position for you EXTRAVERT INTUITIVE
FEELING types... You entrepreneurs. The only troublesome
words here are 'team player' and 'budgetary control'. Your
kind have to be in charge and are usually not happy with
budgetary restrictions unless you can make that
requirement part of the challenge! But you can motivate,
inspire, create, and you love nothing better than challenge.
You get along very well with others as long as they don't try
to tell you how you 'should' do something.

That's an idea of how to read the 'Appointments'
(Help Wanted pages).
The rest is up to you !

GOOD LUCK!

Hiring a new employee can be expensive. Setting up the payroll, the hours, days or maybe even weeks of training before the employee is ready to perform in your organisation costs money. How much would you save if you could be certain that the person you hire will like the job, do it competently and without stress?

By administering the PREFERENTIAL QUESTIONNAIRE to all applicants for any specific job, you can do an initial screening in ten minutes, thus eliminating any whose personality type is not compatible with the job on offer. It is also quite possible that with a reshuffling of presently employed personnel into positions where they will be less stressed and therefore more effective your organisation could run more efficiently and productively. One company with whom I worked shifted a critical **ESTJ** from sales manager to production manager and promoted an **ENFP** sales person to sales manager. Sales tripled in one year.

There is a place in every organisation for all the personality types. The following organisational chart with suggested types for each position may help you select the right person for each job.

RESEARCH & DEVELOPMENT:		**INTJ, ENTJ, INTP, ENTP 's**
		ENFJ,ENTJ,ENTP,ENFP 's
TECHNICAL SERVICES:		**ESTJ, ISTJ, ESTP, ISTP 's**
TROUBLE SHOOTING:		**ESTP, ISTP, ENTP, INTP 's**
PRODUCTION:		**ESTJ, ESFJ, ISTJ, ISFJ 's**
SALES:	of Product	**ESFJ, ESFP 's**
	of Ideas	**ENFJ, ENFP 's**
SECRETARIAL:		**ISFJ, ESFJ 's**
CLERICAL:	People:	**ESFJ, ISFJ 's**
	Machines	**ESTJ, ISTJ 's**
ACCOUNTING:		**ISTJ, ISFJ 's**
PERSONNEL:	Interviewers	**INFJ, INFP 's**

If the job requires organising, analysing, where a critical, logical mind is necessary, but there is little or no dealing with the public, you will want a person scoring high in '**T**-Thinking'.

If the job requires dealing with and getting along with the public, selling, convincing, persuading, or handling complaints, you will want a person with '**F**-Feeling'.

If the job is routine, monotonous, and/or requires remembering a large number of facts, names, numbers etc. keeping files or inventory, you will want a person with '**S**-Sensation'.

If the job requires originality, creativity, independent, unsupervised activity, is challenging with very little routine, you will want a person with **N**-Intuition'.

If the job requires a person who can handle frequent distractions and/or interruptions, can juggle several activities at the same time, and enjoys people and talking on the telephone, or attending conferences, you will want an '**E**-Extravert'.

If the job requires spending large amounts of time alone or with only one or two others, considerable concentration, and has few interruptions, you will want an '**I**- Introvert'. If the job requires constancy, punctuality, and follow-through, you will want a person who scores high in '**J**-Judgement'.

If the job requires adaptability, travel, open - mindedness, little supervision, requires independent action, and results in an immediate reward, you will want a person who scores '**P**- Perceptive'.

In almost any organisation of any size, all the types have a place, but generally speaking, the old adage, "birds of a feather flock together" and "water seeks it's own level" holds true of personality types. Intuitives and sensation types find great difficulty in communicating with each other and thinkers frequently upset feelers because of their perceived lack of tact and sensitivity .

An informed, aware employer with a knowledge of these differences is equipped to avoid unnecessary friction and misunderstanding. A happy employee is a productive employee and that, of course, makes a profit for everyone.

HAPPY HIRING!

Johnson, Robert A. *Ecstacy*, Harper & Row, San Francisco, 1987

Jung, C. G., *Psychological Types*, Harcourt Brace, New York, 1926.

Kiersey, David & Bates, Marilyn, *Please Understand Me*, Prometheus Nemesis Books, Del Mar, 1978.

Myers, Isabel Briggs, *Gifts Differing*, Consulting Psychologists Press Inc. Palo Alto, CA, 1980.

Von Franz, Marie & Hillman, James, *Jung's Typology*, Spring Publications, Zurich, Switzerland, 1971.

Wheelwright, Joseph, MD, *Psychological Types*, C. G. Jung, Institute of San Fransisco Publications.

Dictionary of Occupational Titles, USA Department of Labor.

Occupational Outlook Handbook, USA Department of Labor, Bureau of Labor Statistics.

88

NOTES

Preferential Questionnaire Answer Sheet

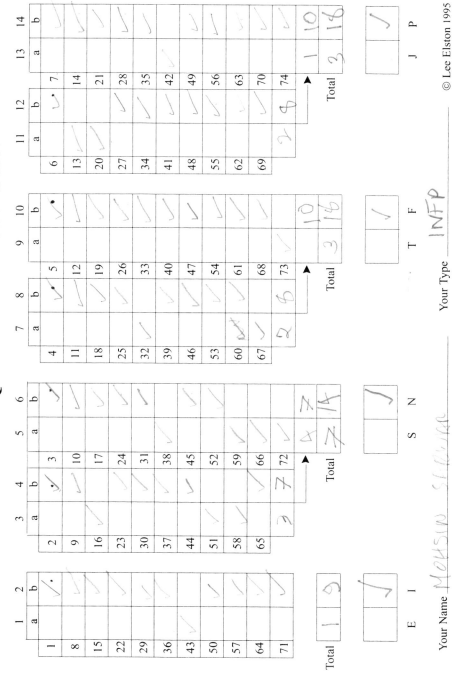

Your Name Mohsin Sullivan

Your Type INFP

Preferential Questionnaire Answer Sheet

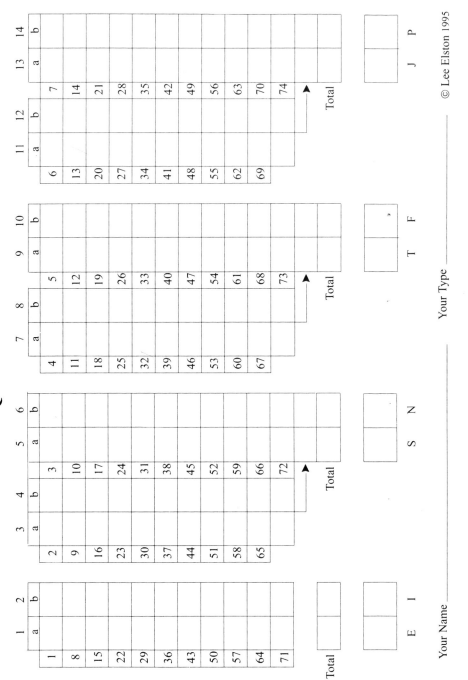

© Lee Elston 1995

Your Name _____   Your Type _____

Preferential Questionnaire Answer Sheet

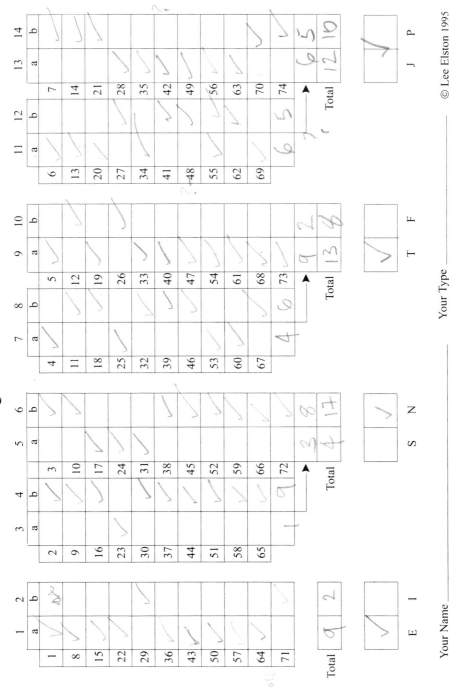

© Lee Elston 1995

Your Name _____

Your Type _____

Preferential Questionnaire Answer Sheet

1 a	2 b
1	
8	
15	
22	
29	
36	
43	
50	
57	
64	
71	

Total

3 a	4 b	5 a	6 b
2	3		
9	10		
16	17		
23	24		
30	31		
37	38		
44	45		
51	52		
58	59		
65	66		
	72		

Total

7 a	8 b	9 a	10 b
4	5		
11	12		
18	19		
25	26		
32	33		
39	40		
46	47		
53	54		
60	61		
67	68		
	73		

Total

11 a	12 b	13 a	14 b
6	7		
13	14		
20	21		
27	28		
34	35		
41	42		
48	49		
55	56		
62	63		
69	70		
	74		

Total

E	I

S	N

T	F

J	P

Your Name _____

Your Type _____

© Lee Elston 1995